HILLTOP SCHOOLS
South Defiance Street
West Unity, Ohio 43570

NATURE RUNS WILD

NATURE RUNS WILD

TRUE DISASTER STORIES

Franklin Watts/New York/London/1979

BY KAREN O'CONNOR SWEENEY

Cover design by Beehive Design Studio, Inc.

Photographs courtesy of: Wide World Photos: pp. 8–9, 18, 22, 44, 48; American Red Cross: pp. 30 (Palmer), 56 (Carland), 70 (Shere), 88 (Smith); Stewart's Photo Shop: p. 32; U.S.D.A. Geological Survey: pp. 34–35; N.O.A.A.: pp. 60, 62; Federal Disaster Assistance Administration: pp. 72, 76; U.S. Army, Defense Civil Preparedness Agency: pp. 74–75; Buffalo Evening News (Ronald J. Calleran): p. 86.

Library of Congress Cataloging in Publication Data

Sweeney, Karen O'Connor.
    Nature runs wild.

    Bibliography: p.
    Includes index.
    SUMMARY: Factual accounts of a variety of natural disasters that have occurred during the last twenty years including the 1964 Alaskan earthquake and the 1977 Buffalo, New York, blizzard.
    1. Natural disasters—Juvenile literature. [1. Natural disasters] I. Title.
GB5019.S93   904'.5   78–7578
ISBN 0–531–02220–X

Copyright © 1979 by Karen O'Connor Sweeney
All rights reserved
Printed in the United States of America
5 4 3

Acknowledgments

The author wishes to thank the following for technical information, advice, suggestions, and photographs:

Ed Diemer, Meteorologist-in-charge, Weather Service Forecast Office, Anchorage, Alaska
John J. Smiles, Chief, Publication Services Branch, National Oceanic and Atmospheric Administration, Rockville, Maryland
Geological Survey, U.S. Department of the Interior
American Red Cross
United States Coast Guard
Buffalo *Courier-Express*
Buffalo *Evening News*
Wide World Photos, Inc., New York
Mrs. Oro Stewart, Stewart's Photo Shop, Anchorage, Alaska
Ginger Scribner, author and friend
Olga Opfell, author and friend
Ross R. Olney, author and friend
Jack Sweeney, husband and friend

And very special thanks to Oscar E. Nichols, Meteorologist and Head Forecaster, National Weather Service Forecast Office, Los Angeles, for reviewing the manuscript for scientific accuracy.

To my friend and colleague
Ross Olney

CONTENTS

Introduction **2**
Freaks of Nature

Chapter One **6**
Avalanche in Peru (1962)

Chapter Two **16**
Volcanic Eruption in Bali (1963)

Chapter Three **28**
Earthquake in Alaska (1964)

Chapter Four **42**
Southern California Flood (1969)

Chapter Five **54**
Great Hurricane Camille (1969)

Chapter Six **68**
Tornado Alley (1974)

Chapter Seven **82**
Blizzard in Buffalo (1977)

Chapter Eight **94**
Predicting Natural Disasters and How to Survive

Chapter Nine **106**
A Look at the Future

Suggestions for Further Reading **114**

Index **115**

NATURE RUNS WILD

INTRODUCTION

FREAKS OF NATURE

On May 31, 1889, a great wall of water rushed down a narrow valley in Johnstown, Pennsylvania. A particularly heavy rain that day caused the largest dam in the world to break. And within an hour, 2,200 people were dead.

On September 8, 1900, in Galveston, Texas, nature struck again. As tourists and townspeople enjoyed the last of summer vacation, an extraordinary storm began to build. People roaming the beaches were fascinated by the unusually high waves. But when wind finally met water, the high tide buried the city, killing 5,000 people. It was one of the worst disasters in the history of North America.

And in San Francisco, California, on April 18, 1906, as citizens slept, the earth below began to rumble and shake. In less than a minute, the city collapsed in ruins. A huge earthquake had ripped open streets, swallowed buildings, destroyed property, and killed about 500 persons.

Those tragedies happened many years ago. People then did not have the necessary information and instruments to help them prepare for emergencies.

Today, however, scientists can sometimes predict natural disasters. And in the future, we may even know enough to protect ourselves from them. But it is doubtful we can ever fully prevent them.

No matter how advanced science becomes, blizzards, floods, volcanic eruptions, earthquakes, hurricanes, and tornadoes will probably continue to occur.

Although an earthquake or a hurricane is different in many ways from a blizzard or avalanche, there are similarities, too. Whenever disaster strikes, no matter what kind it is, people's lives change suddenly.

At first, many victims seem to think they are being "punished" or singled out from the rest. Most are overwhelmed by a sense of fear and aloneness. They feel somehow different from others.

And very often, people act in unusual ways during a disaster. Quiet people may turn into heroes, rescuing children and animals from danger. Talkative people may become scared and shy. And adults may find they are as much in need of comfort as their children.

Survivors are often so upset they can't fully understand what has happened. Some stare at their surroundings in silence. Others panic and begin looking for their lost family and friends.

But after a while, even though death and destruction are all around, most disaster victims are just glad to be alive. They want to get on with their lives. Together they work to repair their homes, businesses, and property. And as strangers become friends, they are reminded of their need for each other. Most begin to appreciate life more. And they learn the value of family and friends.

This book will show what happens when nature strikes. Each of the following chapters features a different kind of natural disaster that has occurred throughout the world in recent times.

Each story is true. And each tells interesting and important facts about how natural forces work, their causes and effects. But perhaps more important, each story shows how people react when nature runs wild.

CHAPTER ONE

AVALANCHE IN PERU (1962)

January 10, 1962, was especially clear in Peru. Just below the peak of its highest mountain, Nevado Huascarán, the late afternoon sun warmed Glacier 511. Drops of melted snow trickled down its icy face.

Beneath the towering 22,000-foot (6,700-meter) peak, the evening chill gradually replaced the afternoon sun. Shepherds pulled ponchos about their shoulders and began to herd their flocks home. The day's chores were almost finished.

In the town of Ranrahirca ("Hill of Many Stones"), people prepared dinner and relaxed with friends and family. Teen-agers clustered in the schoolyard after class, joking and chatting with friends.

In Yungay, as the day drew to a close, Dr. Leoncio Guzmán gazed for a moment at the mountain's snow-capped summit. "I saw a cloud forming and turning golden in the setting sun," he said.

Seconds later, 2½ miles (4 kilometers) overhead, Glacier 511 shuddered. A block of ice, "the size of two Empire State Buildings," weighing nearly 5 million tons (about 4.5 million metric tons), suddenly broke loose.

"When I saw that the cloud was actually flying downhill, I got into my car and drove as fast as I could to Ranrahirca, where my two children were guests at a birthday party."

The doctor had to cover only 6 miles (nearly 10 kilometers), but by the time he got there, the town was already crumbling under the avalanche. "I saw some children running out of the house where my two children were, and then everything went—vanished—like in a nightmare."

The first fall was swift and silent. But as the giant mass of ice crashed into a gorge below, the thundering sound echoed throughout the valley. The roar was "like that of ten thousand wild beasts," recalled one man. "Like an earthquake," said another.

Above the town, a sixty-year-old widow, Zoila Cristina Angel, watched in amazement. "I saw it sweep by like a river," she said, "carrying away one farmer after another. Voices called, 'Run! Run!' but I could not run. I could not move. I could not speak. I just looked at that awful thing that came rushing at us like the end of the world." Fortunately, it passed her by.

It took eight minutes for the avalanche from Glacier 511 to travel the 12 miles (19 kilometers) to Ranrahirca and the surrounding villages. The wild white carpet, 1½ miles (2.5 kilometers) wide and as thick as 40 feet (12 meters), smothered the red-tiled roofs, buried farmlands and bridges, and drenched the cobbled streets.

As it crashed down the slope, great heavy clouds of finely ground snow rose into the air and were carried far out from the actual path of the speeding river of snow.

Ice or *summer* avalanches like this occur when great masses of ice thaw and detach themselves from high glaciers during warm weather. When these masses become too heavy for their support, as happened on Glacier 511, they break loose and crash to lower levels. This is known as a *sliding* avalanche.

Even daily examinations from the air, for breaks and weak spots in dangerous mountain snowfields, cannot completely guard against an avalanche. No one can predict for sure when the snow masses will move. Any vibrations in the air can trigger the onslaught. A scouting plane, an unwary skier, an unusual wind may set the snow sheet in action.

With the wave of snow and ice came millions of tons of boulders, trees, and mud, resulting in one of the endless *huaycos* (landslides) that are associated with life on the slopes of the Andes Mountains. The thundering mass spilled into the Ranrahirca River at the head of the valley, burying

A Peruvian Air Force photo shows the path of the devastating 1962 avalanche.

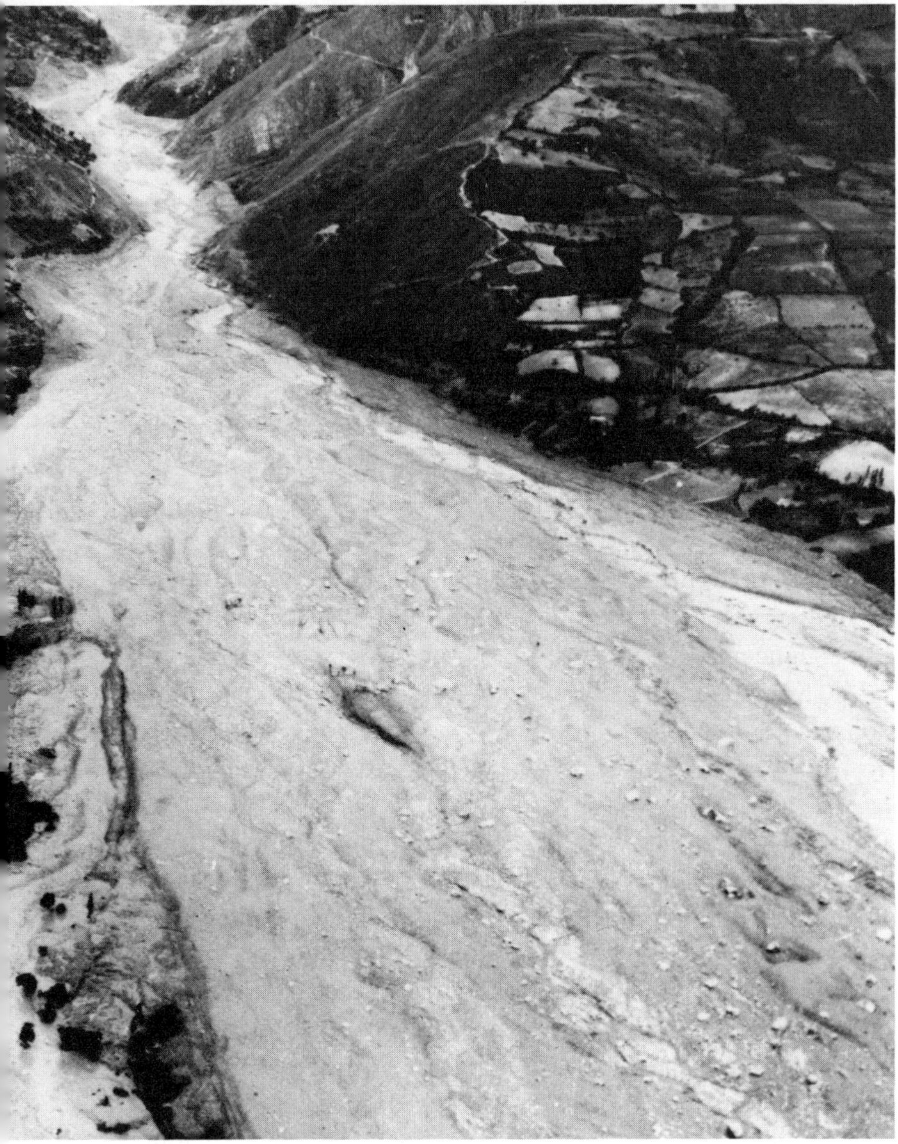

forever twelve villages and hamlets and nearly all of their residents. It traveled faster than a railway express and took so short a time to reach the valley that escape was almost impossible.

The powder from the ice proved more dangerous than earth dust because it quickly suffocated the people in its path. It melted in their lungs in seconds and filled them with water. There were no serious injuries. People either escaped completely or were buried alive, as the white death erased everything in its course.

There were many conditions that contributed to this avalanche. But those that made it deadly were the lack of warning and the amazing speed. The physical properties of the snow itself were also important.

Snow can be dry and fluffy like down or moist and compacted like damp salt. The action of the sun, rain and wind, the temperature and humidity, and the age of the snow are also significant.

Three types of snow make up the layers on a mountain slope:

Wild snow—This is snow that falls freely from cold air ($14°$ F to $-4°$ F; $-10°$ C to $-20°$ C). It forms a cover over a mountain area and usually contains about 98 percent air. This *powder* or *fluffy* snow is an example of the early stages of much of the snow that gathers on cold mountain slopes before the cover settles.

Packed snow—Containing about 78 percent air, packed snow is a mass of snow crystals cemented to one another and formed into tough crusts by the action of the sun or wind.

Old snow (firn)—This is composed of sugar-like granules whose particles are sometimes cube-shaped. It is so compacted that only 20 to 50 percent is air. In the spring, on moderately steep slopes, old snow starts to creep slowly, depending on the surface.

But the most important single factor that influences an avalanche is the *anchorage*—the conditions that hold the snow in place on the slope. Anchorage depends on the texture of the surface of the mountain. Some surfaces are rough like sandpaper. Others may be as slick as typing paper. To illustrate, a mound of sand will rapidly slide off typing paper that is pinned to a slant board. But the same sand will spill from the sandpaper at a much slower rate because of the rough base.

Smooth rock and grassy slopes, like slick paper, are poor footholds for snow covers. And uneven timber and brush grounds, like sandpaper, usually offer better anchorage.

When the sun and wind crust over the top layer of existing snow, this slick surface makes an effective ramp or slide. As new blankets of fluffy snow fall, they lie lightly on the slick crust. Just one additional snowfall is generally all that's needed to make up the necessary weight of crystals to cause an avalanche of the entire cover.

A more moist snowfall will provide better anchorage, but only until the wind and sun melt it and force it down the slippery mountainside.

The basic cause of all avalanches is heavy snowfall. The weight of one layer on top of another produces stress within and causes deep cracks to form. Once the snow sheet is broken, the downward pressure of the snow on the slope overcomes the anchorage, and an avalanche is on its way.

The avalanche in Peru in 1962 was no exception. The ingredients were just right. Unusually warm weather followed a freak snowfall.

Besides Ranrahirca and its many surrounding villages,

the avalanche reached the Santa River as well, and dammed it. As the water rose 15 feet (4.5 meters), debris and ice floated downstream. The flood had wiped out bridges to the towns of Yungay and Caras. The government hoped to airlift supplies to the isolated townspeople. But the landing strip was narrow and the rainy season threatened its use.

Looking at the pitiful remains of Ranrahirca, Mayor Alfonso Caballero, one of the town's ninety-eight survivors, said, "I don't know why I didn't go mad."

"Looking toward the village, I saw only a waste of mud and ice," added one lonely man. "Realizing that my wife, my children, and my parents were all buried under the debris, I suddenly found myself sobbing."

Every inch of land was a reminder of the horror. The grotesque and twisted bodies of the dead were everywhere. Some were found 100 miles (160 kilometers) away, where the Santa River empties into the Pacific Ocean. Most of the dead were not recognizable. Heads, arms, legs had been torn from their torsos.

As men and equipment began digging through the mounds of mud and slush, more and more bodies were recovered. Each day the bulldozers progressed. "In a few weeks," one engineer said, "the road will be restored across the avalanche path."

The morgue was the saddest place of all. Some 3,500 people were killed in the disaster. Many were never unearthed from the mud and rubble. Hundreds, however, were found and brought for burial. Thirty-six coffins held parts of about 130 bodies.

One father found his son there, a yo-yo hanging from one pocket. "Homero was my youngest," the father said, as he gently undressed the boy and washed his face in a final gesture of love. "Homero was ten years old," he added, and lifted his son to a bed of boxes for burial.

President Kennedy of the United States offered assistance, but little help was needed. There were almost no people injured. Those who did survive turned Inés Colegio High School into a refugee center. And some 400 survivors ate lunch together on the patio.

The Peruvian Air Force had flown in three small French helicopters for distributing blankets, clothes, food, and medical supplies, where needed. And the Army engineers began building temporary footbridges out of wooden scraps of rubble.

As devastating as the avalanche had been, it was not the first time Peruvians had faced the white death. In 1941, just 30 miles (48 kilometers) from Ranrahirca, another avalanche at Huarás claimed the lives of 5,000 citizens.

Disasters even more deadly have struck around the world. In 1920, 200,000 Chinese were killed in one of the worst avalanches in history. The most common belt in the world for avalanches, however, is in the Alps Mountains in Europe. The loss of life was particularly high on the Austro-Italian frontier during the First World War, in 1916, where 6,000 military men were victims of another avalanche.

Gradually the people of Peru adjusted to their losses. They did what had to be done. And Mayor Caballero supported the citizens in their efforts to rebuild.

"I have made a proclamation," he said. "We will build a new town—the site will be chosen soon." He decided to call the new town after the old—Ranrahirca, the Hill of Many Stones. And the main avenue would carry the memory of that terrifying day forever. It would be called the Street of January Tenth.

CHAPTER TWO

VOLCANIC ERUPTION IN BALI (1963)

Between Southeast Asia and Australia, on the beautiful island of Bali, the natives hold a religious festival once every hundred years. (A Balinese year has 210 days.) They follow the Hindu belief that nature sometimes becomes unbalanced by human sins. Only a ceremony of prayer and sacrifice, called Eka Dasa Rudra, can restore it to order.

Worshipers prepare this sacred festival to make up for their sins. They pray and dance for the gods and offer them delicacies of rice, bamboo shoots, fried cakes, barbecued meats, and bowls of bananas and other tropical fruits.

In March of 1963, as villagers gathered in the sacred temple of Besakih, this once-a-century feast was coming to a close. It had begun five months earlier at the foot of Gunung Agung, "Navel of the World." Stretching 10,308 feet (3,140 meters) above sea level, it is the highest volcanic peak on the island.

Just a month before, the mighty mountain, home of the gods to the Balinese, had stirred after napping for more than one hundred years. Loud underground rumblings, perhaps due to the movement of gases under pressure, warned the natives of the coming danger. Then, on March 12, mud and stones began to flow down the southeast side of Agung. A sudden shower of smoke and brimstone killed seventeen people.

As the mountain shuddered and smoked, the Balinese people believed the gods were angry. The trembling earth and boiling crater must be punishment for their sins, they thought. Thousands rushed to mountainside shrines to pray. They begged the gods to rid the land of ghosts and demons, and to save them from this disaster. But no one moved off the island. They believed their prayers would be answered.

The Balinese were unaware that, some 20 to 30 miles (some 30 to 48 kilometers) below the volcano, extremely hot melted rock, called *magma,* had begun to force its way to the top. The magma, containing much gas, made up chiefly of steam or water vapor, pushed against the melting roof of its compartment and released the underground gases.

For reasons not yet clear to scientists, some of the rocks in the upper crust of the earth are hot. This heat may be due to radioactivity. Granite, for example, a common rock on the continents, contains some radioactive minerals. The breaking down of these minerals might produce enough heat to melt the rocks.

We can't be certain of the cause of the heat, but we do know that there is an increasing degree of heat as we go deeper and deeper into the mine shafts and oil wells of the earth. This increase in temperature at greater depths is called *geothermal gradient*.

During a volcanic eruption, the boiling hot rocks exert a tremendous explosive pressure on their surroundings. And before long, they reach the weaker places in the earth's outer crust, in search of a place to escape. A passage called a *conduit* is then blasted through the earth's surface, and the explosive gases and rocks rush through it to the outside.

Just after sunrise on March 17, 1963, the action of the gas in the upper part of Mount Agung caused this kind of gigantic eruption. The powerful mountain suddenly blew its top. As the magma spilled from the opening, it cooled, turned to lava, then flowed over the outside of the crater until it hardened.

Within minutes, a blanket of the boiling lava and burning ash smothered 125,000 acres (50,600 hectares) of greenery and killed more than 1,500 of the world's gentlest people. The fire and fury of the volcanic eruption turned the island paradise into a black wilderness.

For some time to come, Balinese women in colorful sarongs would no longer stroll the quiet streets balancing fruit

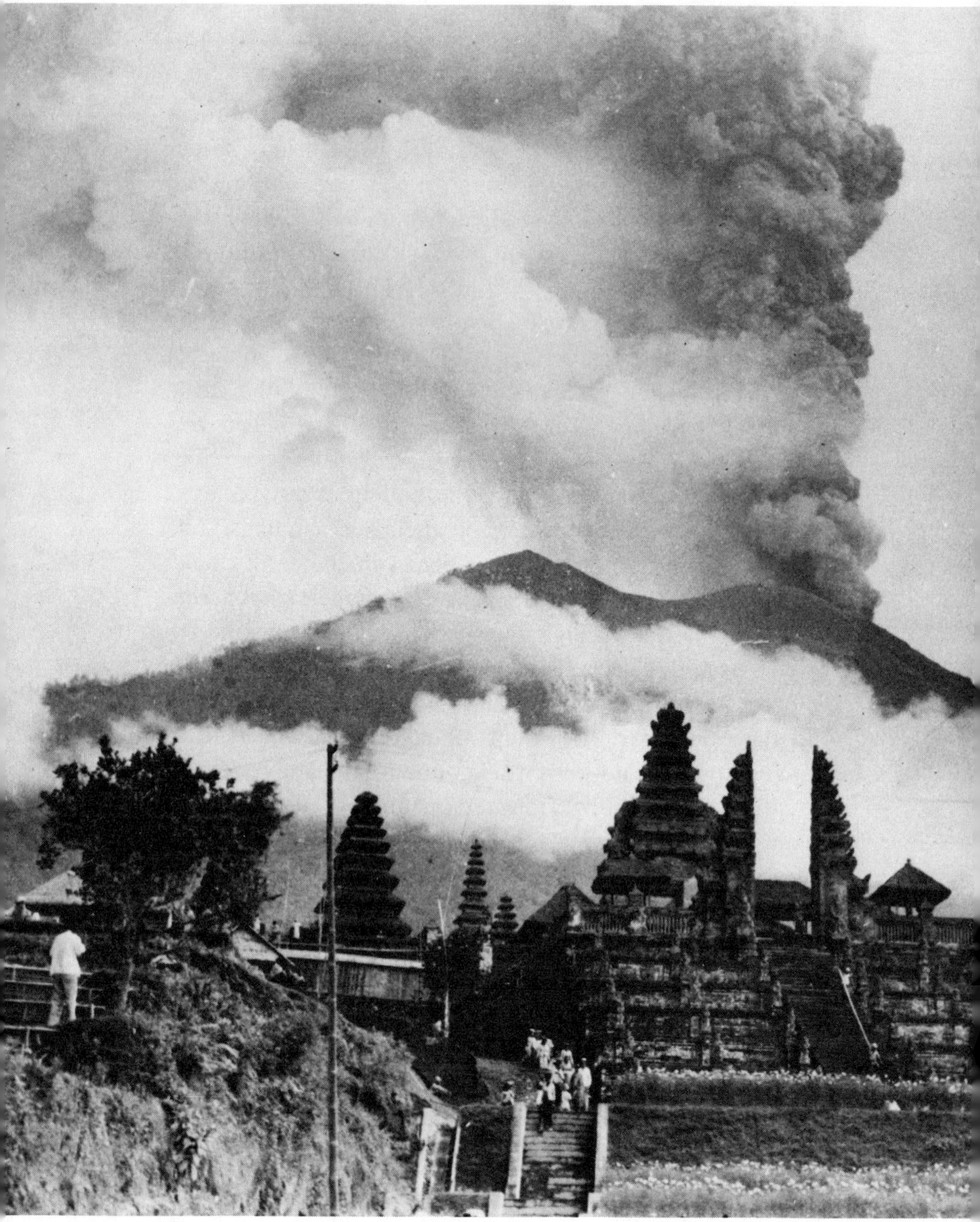

baskets and water jars on their heads. Straw-hatted men would not be seen trotting evenly under the heavy shoulder poles that held their food and supplies. And merry Balinese children with almond eyes and light brown skin could no longer play in the green rice fields.

"Suddenly it was dark," one twenty-five-year-old man, named Sepek, reported later. "I ran out of the temple, but a hot cloud came toward us. I went back and prayed with the others."

At first, there was no noise. People simply stared at the heavy black cloud overhead, caused by a mixture of steam and extremely fine dust. Then all at once came the *duk-duk-duk* of falling stone. Pieces of rock were thrown into the air from the crust around the cone of the volcano and from deep within the conduit.

Volcanic ash, lapilli (small stones), and *volcanic cinders,* each a different kind of hardened lava, exploded from the mouth of the volcano. And there were also larger pieces of hot lava, called *volcanic bombs,* which cooled when they reached the air. Some, as big as 15 feet (4.5 meters) in length, beat down on the temple. Sepek tried to awaken some of the worshipers, but there was no answer. Most had died immediately.

According to one scientist, many of the victims were killed by clouds of explosive gases that were mixed with crushed ash and lava. The fiery clouds had swept down the mountainside at terrific speed, burning everything in their

Mount Agung spewing a pillar of smoke before its eruption in March 1963.

path. Even the children did not cry out. They could make only strange wailing sounds because their mouths were filled with ashes.

Sepek rushed out of the stone temple when the curled roof caught fire. As he raced through the hot coals, his legs and arms began to burn, and he quickly covered his face with part of his clothing.

Without stopping, the frightened young man ran 9 miles (14.5 kilometers) to warn the people in the town of Selat. A village doctor treated his burns with tea, then sent him down the mountain in a car. Fortunately, Sepek's wife and child were safe. They had left town two hours before the hot cloud came.

The following day, a shower of volcanic gravel rained down on mountainside villages. The salt-and-pepper-colored mixture reached as far as 30 miles (48 kilometers) from the mouth of the volcano. And waves of *lahar* (boiling mud and ash) swept down the volcano under heavy rains, turning rivers black and wild. The dark, rushing waters carried away bridges and buried rice fields in muck.

In the days that followed, the sickening smell of sulfur hung in the air. There was barely a sound, as pigs, chickens, geese, and ducks lay dead all around. The ground was too hot to touch. Frightened citizens searched for their missing relatives. And starved-looking dogs prowled through the ruins whining for food.

Homeless survivors huddled together in thatched huts. But the shelter was poor and there was too little food. Many waited in fear for word about their families. "I have not seen my wife and children since Agung became angry," one man said. "Where they are I don't know."

One group of villages to the east of Besakih was destroyed so swiftly and so completely that, even two weeks later, officials couldn't be sure what happened. A deadly black cloud of burning 230° F (110° C) ash had roasted hundreds of worshipers where they knelt.

Hospitals took in badly burned men, women, and children. But the number was so great that many went without blankets, bandages, and beds.

One lame, blind young man, barely alive, was discovered nine days after the explosion by a patrol led by two Indonesian volcanologists. They got him to a hospital just in time to save his life.

In other parts of the island, long lines of people crossed the river carrying their belongings on their backs. Some clustered in town squares waiting for supplies to arrive by helicopter. They received about a pound of corn or rice a day. "This is barely enough to prevent starvation," a doctor stated, "but it is all we can give them. There is no more."

Bali's governor, Anak Agung Sutedja, later said, "We have to feed 77,000 refugees and we simply have not got the food to do it."

The eruption had permanently ruined more than 25,000 acres (10,100 hectares) of farmland. And an additional 100,000 acres (40,500 hectares) could not be planted for many years. Subagan, for example, a town of many fine buildings, was buried in black ash and mud. Two hundred of its 5,000 residents had been swept away as they prayed in their temple. They had barely heard the rumble of boiling mud before the end came.

Indonesia's President Sukarno declared Bali a disaster area and promised assistance. Help arrived from other lands, as well. The United States Embassy in Djakarta, the capital of Indonesia, sent three planeloads of medical supplies. The Netherlands, Great Britain, Italy, India, Japan, Australia, and the United Nations offered relief. And a team of doctors and

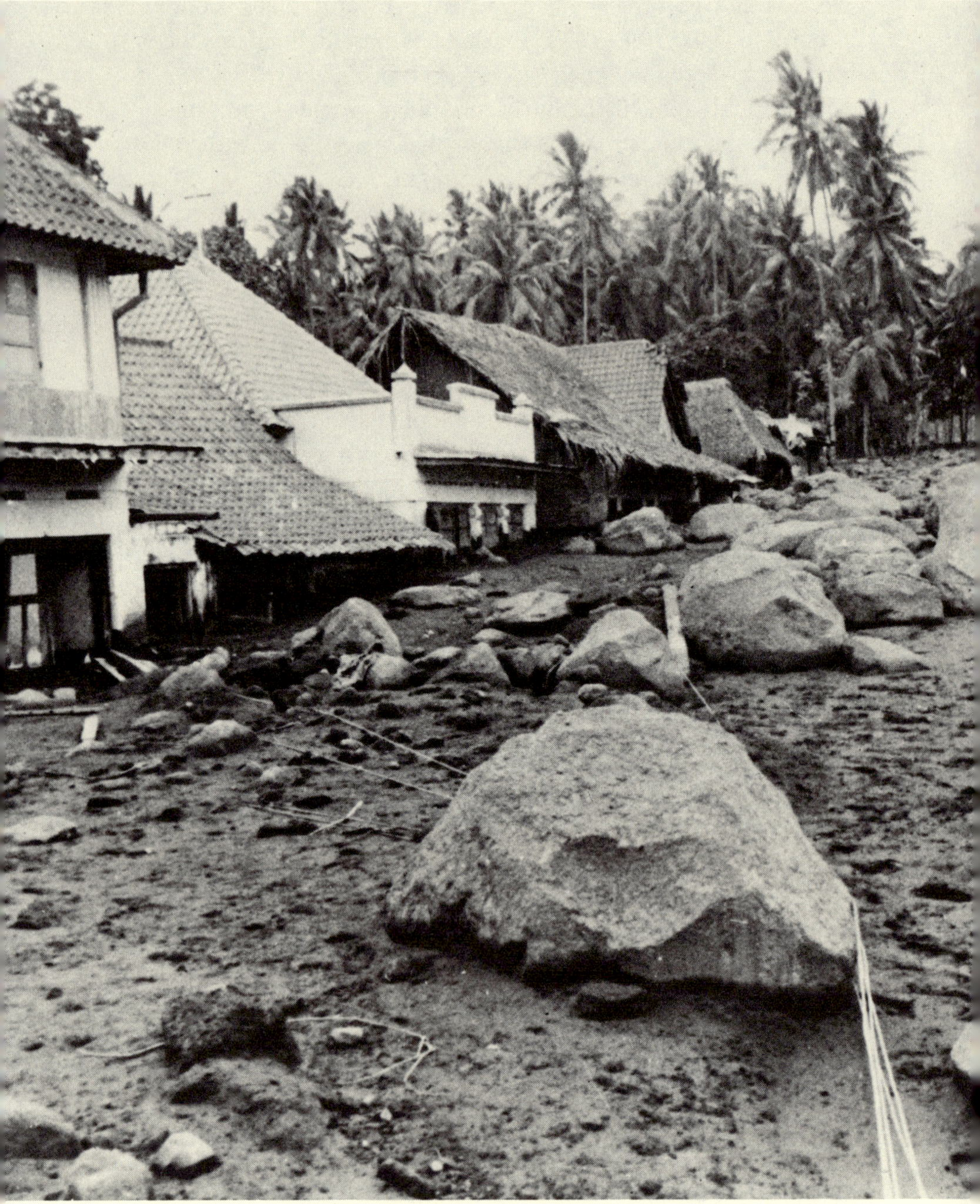

paramedics from the Philippines flew in and set up medical aid stations.

Even though the destruction of Bali was far-reaching, it was not an entirely new experience for its people. The Balinese had learned to live with uncertainty, for the Indonesian islands are located in a part of the world called the *ring of fire*. These areas of weakness in the earth's crust are generally along the seacoast and near the great mountain chains.

This famous volcanic zone goes around the Pacific Ocean to the Atlantic through Central and South America, to Antarctica, and up the western side of the Pacific from New Zealand and Indonesia to the Philippines, Japan, and Kamchatka. A few of the volcanic eruptions in these locations occur under the sea. But unless they reach the surface, they are not likely to be noticed by people.

Some volcanoes are constantly *active*. Others are *intermittent*, erupting at fairly regular periods. And still others are *dormant*, or resting. This means they have not been dead long enough for us to know when they will break out again. That was the case with Mount Agung. It had been still since 1843. Volcanoes that have remained quiet since the beginning of recorded history are considered *extinct*.

Although help came from many directions, the destruction in Bali in 1963 was so great that much of the aid was held up because of transportation problems. Every inch of land appeared to be bathed in warm soft mud. Giant boul-

Lava, mud, and boulders that have moved down the slopes of the erupting Mount Agung volcano fill the streets of a Balinese village.

ders, the size of houses, blocked most passageways. Driving was nearly impossible.

In Tianjar, on the northern coast of Bali, lava continued to pour from the crater. "That lava is nearly 250 feet [76 meters] thick and 400° Fahrenheit [204° Celsius] at its base," reported a volcanologist, Mr. Soerjo, whose job was to keep watch on Mount Agung. Later, he was to study its crater, but that couldn't be done safely for at least two months, he commented. An avalanche of ash could be triggered easily, and if rain should come, too, it would turn into a boiling mudflow that could wipe out everything in its path.

"It could happen again," he said, referring to the eruption. "That's why we have recommended that everyone within 10 kilometers [6 miles] from the crater be evacuated."

But when Governor Sutedja closed the area to residents, he faced a difficult problem. "Besakih is our mother temple, the holiest in Bali," he said. "We have not had much trouble in persuading villagers to leave their homes, but the priests do not like to leave the temples—particularly Besakih."

But in Lebih, one of the villages highest on the mountain, the people were reluctant to leave their homes because they believed they were the servants of Mount Agung. It was difficult to get them to move because, as one doctor said, "without the great mountain, there would be nothing in life for these people."

On the day of the April full moon, with one of the last important ceremonies of the Eka Dasa Rudra due to take place, the governor announced that Besakih would be forbidden to the people. He said that he alone would go to the temple to pray for the entire island.

But on the holy day itself, he found himself watching hopelessly as long lines of worshipers trudged up the mountain to the temple. There was nothing he could do to keep them away. But there was one small sign of hope. For the first time in a week, the sky looked clear.

And so the ceremonies continued while Mount Agung smoked quietly in the background. But even as the Balinese people prayed, the volcano only rested.

Mr. Soerjo's predictions were to be proved correct. "It could happen again," he had warned. And just a few weeks later, on May 16, the mighty Mount Agung erupted again. More than 100 persons were killed. And much property was damaged. But halfway up the fiery slope, untouched by the death and destruction around it, the many-towered temple of Besakih was still standing.

CHAPTER THREE

EARTHQUAKE IN ALASKA (1964)

Snow fell on Anchorage, Alaska. The thermometer registered 24° F (−4° C). It was Good Friday, March 27, 1964, two days before Easter.

Despite the freezing temperatures, however, there was a holiday feeling in the air. Schools were closed for spring vacation. Many people had worshiped at the traditional three-hour Good Friday service at church. And some had shopped at the new and popular Penney's Department Store. By evening, most residents were on their way home.

But as they moved through the city's streets, they had no way of knowing that, 18 miles (29 kilometers) beneath the earth's thin, changeable crust, two rock masses had begun to slip against one another.

Just as a safety valve releases excess pressure from a boiler, nature was preparing to unleash the dangerous forces that had built up in the spinning earth below Alaska.

At 5:30 P.M., Paula Slaymaker, a fourteen-year-old student at Ora Dee Clark Junior High School, and her mother drove to their home on the east side of Anchorage. Suddenly, without warning, their car began backing down the level driveway by itself!

And as the earth's unsteady innards continued to rumble and stir, Robert Girt, in his apartment on Sixteenth Avenue, dropped the shoes he was shining. All at once, the earth's crust exploded. "It's a quake," he thought half-aloud.

In another part of town, Attorney Russell Arnett, leaving his clothes behind, burst out of the Athletic Club steam bath and charged down the street.

In the community of Turnagain, at the southeast district of Anchorage, Mr. J. D. Peters walked out to meet his wife as she pulled into the driveway. All at once the ground began to shake.

At that moment, pressure at the center of the earth had

built up to nearly 50 million pounds per square inch (3.5 million kilograms per square centimeter). This, together with the earth's spinning on its axis at more than 1,000 miles (1,600 kilometers) per hour, made it almost certain that, as one scientist put it, "something had to give!" At that moment, it did just that.

"Come on, honey," Mr. Peters yelled to his wife. But as he stretched out his hand toward her, the driveway opened between them. They faced each other across a gaping hole. Mr. Peters ran to the garage and grabbed an extension cord. He tried to throw it to his wife, but it wouldn't reach. And before he could think what to do next, his house reared like an angry mule and slid toward the sea.

"Hang on!" Peters shouted. Next, as suddenly as it had opened, the giant gap closed, and his wife came sliding across to him.

This earthquake, like others throughout history, occurred along a *fault*. It is the line where rock layers—plates or slabs of the earth's crust—break, bump, and slide by each other.

Geologists, professionals who specialize in earth science, refer to these rock layers or plates in the *plate tectonics theory*. There are about seven major plates in the earth. And as they slowly move past each other, they create stresses that lead to earthquakes. Some scientists compare this rock movement to the stretching and releasing of a rubber band. Geologists, in fact, call it *elastic rebound*. When this rebound takes place, a great deal of energy is released in the form of vibrations called *seismic waves*. There are three kinds of seismic waves—L (large), P (primary), and S (secondary).

The L waves usually begin at the *epicenter*, the point directly above the *focus*, or place of rock movement. They move along the earth's surface and do the greatest damage.

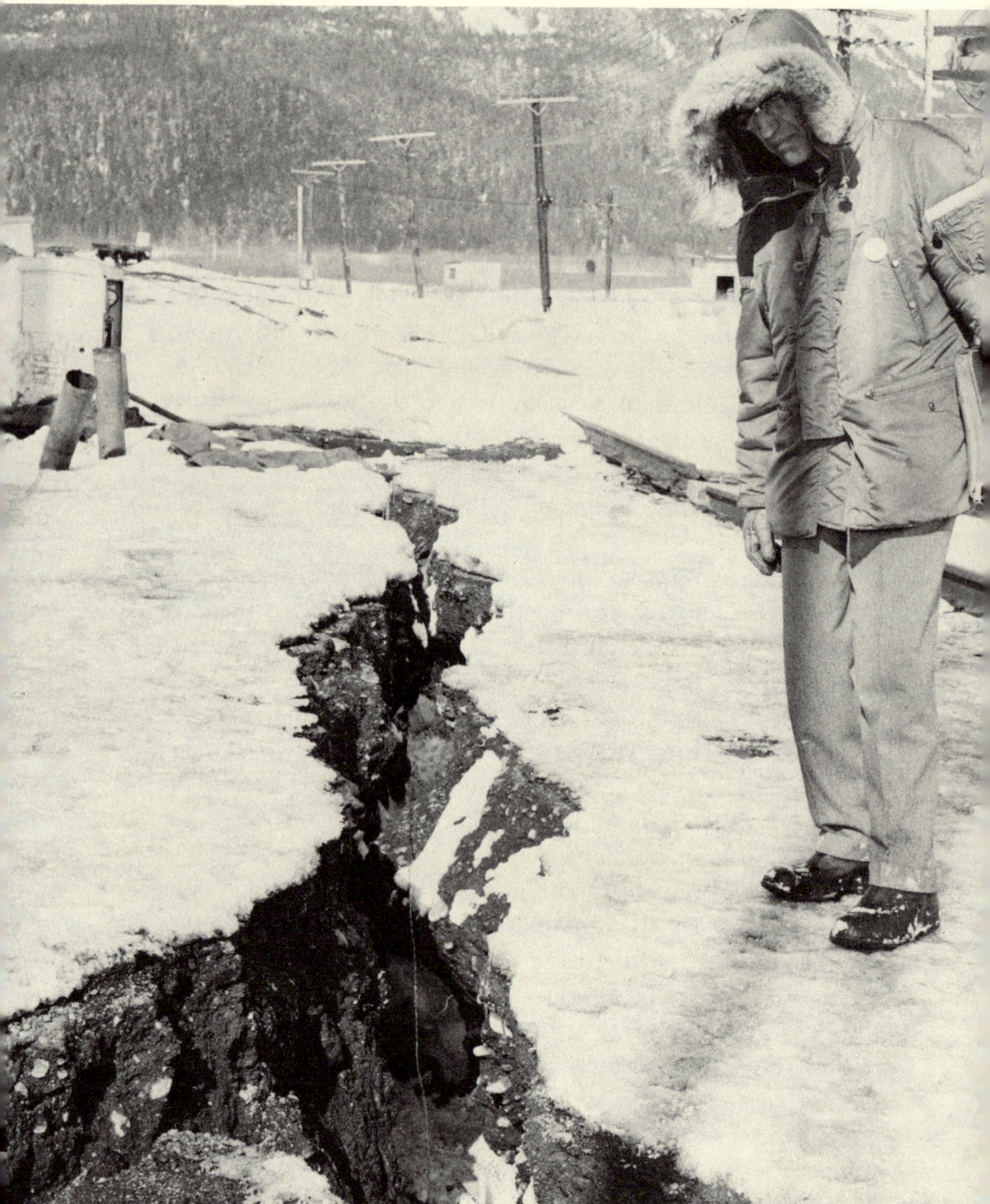

In Alaska, for example, the *L* waves tore at hillsides, destroyed highways, crumbled buildings, and turned smooth streets into a mass of ugly bulges and cracks. But as the *L* waves move away from the *epicenter* of an earthquake, they spread out like ripples in a pond and gradually diminish.

The *P* and *S* waves travel below the earth's surface. They are charted on an instrument called a *seismograph*. This pendulum-like machine records the waves with squiggly lines on a strip of moving paper.

Earthquake scientists, known as *seismologists,* can tell how far an earthquake is from the seismograph station. And with special charts and maps to guide them, they can learn exactly when and where an earthquake took place.

On that March afternoon in 1964, hundreds of seismologists all over the world watched in amazement as their seismographs went crazy. Vibrations were so intense that recording needles went clear off the paper!

Little did the crowd who had gathered at the dock in the city of Valdez, Alaska, know they would make history just minutes later. They watched as the S.S. *Chena,* an Alaska Steamship Company coastal freighter, pulled into shore.

Fourteen-year-old Helen Irish and her girl friends Cheryl Flickenger and Wanda Day were among them. Everyone watched as the ship's forklift hoisted some oil barrels out of the hold and set them down. The girls lingered a few minutes

An American Red Cross disaster worker peers into one of the many crevices created by the March 1964 "Good Friday" earthquake in Anchorage, Alaska.

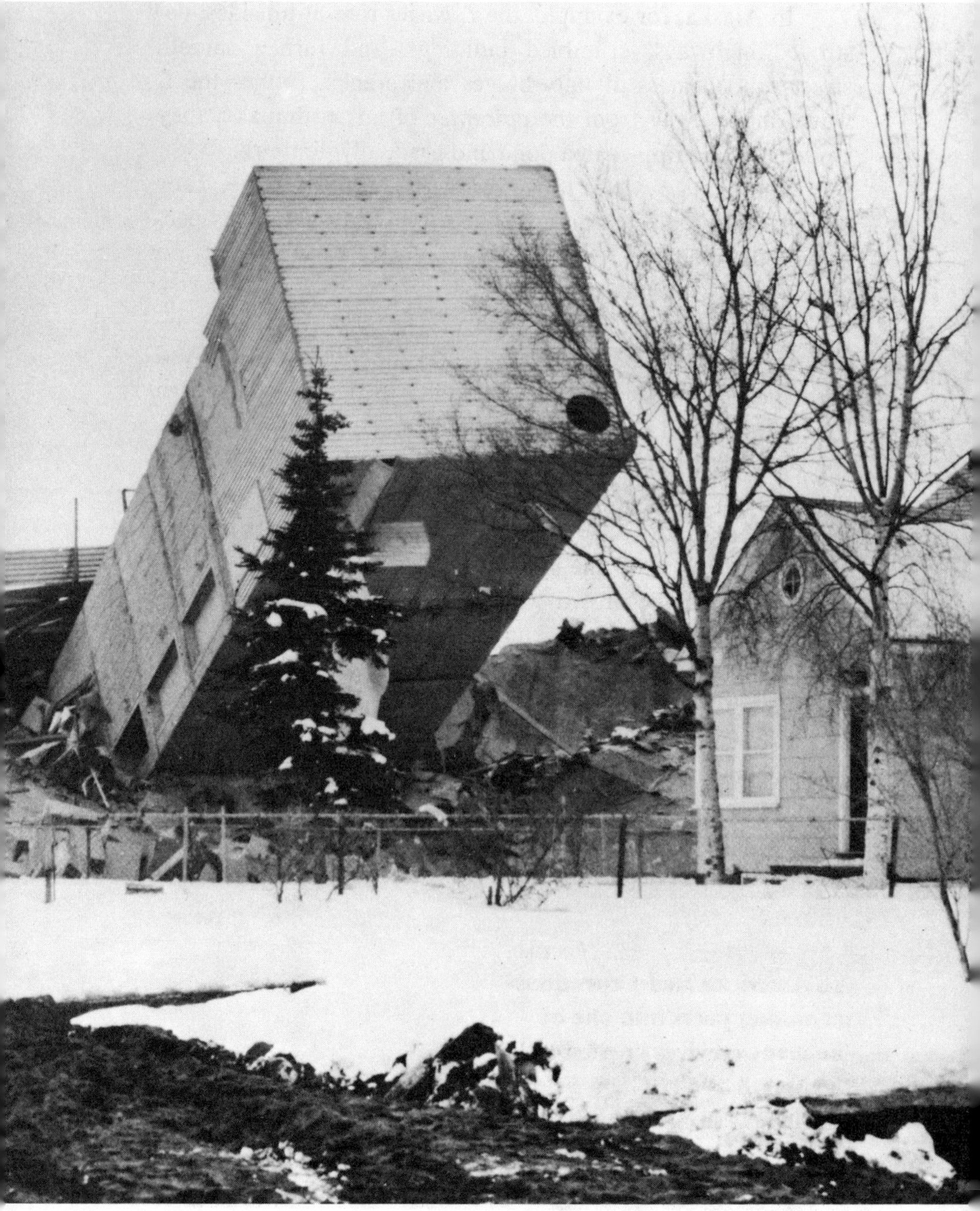

longer, laughing and talking about the teen club dance that night. Then Helen hurried home for dinner.

As her father walked in from work, the tremor began. "All of a sudden the whole earth started shaking like crazy," Helen said later.

"I screamed at my father and ran outside. The ground just opened up. Every time I took a step, I fell into a crevice. The sewage lines in front of our house broke and I had to wade through muck up to my waist.

"I looked down the street and saw the water. It picked up the *Chena* and tossed it like I used to toss boats in the bathtub. The two-story warehouse went flying up and crashed down in the water and disappeared. People on the dock were running, but the water just rose up and swamped them. Dozens of people floated away . . . they just floated away."

Helen's father had gone out to look for her mother. "I nearly died of worry," she said. "I didn't know where my parents were or even if they were still alive. I just sat and shivered."

Meanwhile, young Robert Girt had no time to think about his half-polished shoes. He and his father didn't take any chances. They began leading the two younger children out of the apartment. Suddenly everything went to pieces. Plaster fell. The building swayed back and forth violently. Quickly Girt's family rushed down the fire stairs and ran outside into the street.

Then Robert Girt fought his way back into the building.

A garden apartment complex is twisted apart during the March 1964 earthquake in Anchorage.

The downtown area of Anchorage following the 1964 earthquake.

First, he dragged an old woman to safety. Next, he rammed into a locked apartment and saved an eighty-three-year-old man. And finally, choking and gasping for breath, he smashed through jammed doors, saving a screaming woman and another elderly man. Then, at last, he rescued his sister's cat, who was cowering in a closet.

And as Attorney Arnett flew down Fourth Avenue, a chain of people began to form. Each one was linked to another for protection against the huge holes in the ground. Arnett ran up and latched onto the last one in line. No one seemed to notice that he was naked.

In less than five minutes, three-fourths of Anchorage and Valdez were destroyed. The docks had disappeared. Boats had been smashed and cars crushed. People rushed out of their homes looking for safety. Some drove over the torn streets. And helicopters shuttled others to Glennallen High School, where rescue teams were setting up army cots and food.

Between 5:36 and 5:41 P.M., 200,000 megatons of energy had been released—more than that contained in over a thousand hydrogen bombs. Property damage estimates ranged from $300 to $750 million. One hundred fifteen people died, and 4,500 were left homeless.

Even though the earth continually quivers, and some 5,000 earthquakes are recorded every year, only about 100 are considered major. And the Alaskan earthquake of 1964 was among the worst in history.

The location of the state had a lot to do with the impact. This quake and other major quakes usually occur in two places in the world. One is the rim of the Pacific Ocean, known as the *ring of fire,* which includes Alaska, Japan, and California. The other follows the high mountains from Portugal to Burma. There are also less dangerous earthquakes that run through a range of mountains in the center of the Atlantic Ocean.

To give people a better understanding of how earthquakes affect our lives and property, and the very land we live on, a seismologist named Charles Francis Richter worked out a way to measure the amount of energy that is released from earthquakes. It is called the *Richter scale*. Depending on the intensity of the vibrations, each earthquake is given a number from 1 to 10. The higher the number, the greater the intensity.

The Richter scale works something like this:

RICHTER SCALE	EFFECTS
1	Picked up only on the seismograph
2	Usually picked up only on the seismograph
3	Noticed and felt by only a few people
4	Similar to the vibrations of a passing bus or truck
5	Plates and cups fall from shelves, light fixtures sway
6	Walls crack, chimneys break, bricks tumble
7	Pipes crack, some buildings collapse, landslides occur
8 and over	Ground erupts and shifts; objects get tossed into air

Scientists record the seismic waves, or vibrations, at their stations. Then several readings are compared before a number is assigned. Going up by one number means that the quake is ten times as big, or as intense, as the number just below it.

The Alaskan earthquake registered 8.5 on the Richter scale. The ground vibrations, however, were not the only cause of destruction. The town of Seward, just south of Anchorage, was also hit hard by the first *tsunami* (a Japanese word meaning "storm or harbor wave"), caused by an undersea earthquake, sometimes called a *seaquake*. As the rock beneath the ocean shifts, the sea floor heaves and plunges, setting millions of tons of water into motion.

Within minutes of the first jolt on land, this great wall of water swept across the Pacific Ocean at thundering speed. As boats and houses quickly disappeared, it rushed on, nearly wiping out the village of Chenega.

Then warnings flashed, as it moved south and west at 500 miles (800 kilometers) per hour. But they did not come soon enough for some people. One family of four children and their parents drowned as they slept on an Oregon beach.

The wave continued down the Pacific coast and finally crashed on the shore of Crescent City, California, on the Oregon border, more than 2,000 miles (3,200 kilometers) from the original site.

"We have been subject to no heavier blow," said Alaska's Governor William Egan. Within hours, relief was on its way. The Air Force flew in a mobile hospital with supplies of every kind. And Governor Egan also requested emergency funds from President Johnson. "It is the only way we can rebuild," he said.

By the next morning, however, things began to mend slowly for the fortunate survivors.

Robert Girt, safe with his family, could once again give some thought to polishing his shoes.

Helen Irish's tears turned to smiles when she found her mother asleep on an army cot at Glennallen High School.

The Peterses were safe and happy to be alive, even though they had lost their home and Mr. Peters had broken three ribs.

And Attorney Arnett, though he had lost his house, found his family to be all right, and, thank heaven, someone had given him some clothes to wear!

CHAPTER FOUR

SOUTHERN CALIFORNIA FLOOD (1969)

The sun always shines in Southern California, the land of backyard swimming pools, teen-age surfers, and sandy beaches. California was truly the "golden state"—until January 19, 1969, when residents experienced one of the worst floods and mudslides in the history of the state.

Except for a few clear periods, the remainder of the month was cloudy or partly cloudy, and it continued that way into February. Southern Californians learned what it was like to be wet, soaked, drenched—nearly drowned in water. And for many it was a scary experience.

As Edward Jennings drove along the Pomona Freeway, a mysterious force suddenly grabbed his car and pushed it sideways onto the center strip. The cliff above had collapsed.

"I hadn't seen the landslide come down," he said, "and I felt as though I were in a boat being tossed about in a storm."

Ralph D. Helfer's ranch—Africa, U.S.A.—home of many famous movie and television animals, was drenched by the Santa Clara River. Several of Mr. Helfer's great beasts were suddenly free to roam neighboring areas where some 10,000 people lived. Fortunately, there was little panic because most people didn't realize what was happening. Communications had broken down.

"When the water reached the cages," Mr. Helfer reported, "we tranquilized the untamed animals. Unfortunately, we lost a dozen lions, tigers, and a jaguar when a dam burst before we could carry them out."

After that they rescued their gentle animals, mostly lions and tigers. They had been patiently tamed with kindness and were no more dangerous than Great Danes.

"The river had made an island of their cage area," said Mr. Helfer. "We reached it by forming a human chain." Mr. Helfer and his men opened the cage doors and called the animals to follow.

"Then came the only beautiful thing in our catastrophe. Together the men and the wonderful animals struggled to save each other. The men provided the leadership, the animals the power to overcome the current while the men clung to their fur. All were saved."

The animals remained quiet while the men made some temporary quarters for them. They could have run away in all the noise and confusion. "But they didn't," said Mr. Helfer. "They wanted to be near their human friends."

The Los Angeles Basin, a former farmland, surrounded by mountains, received a record 25 inches (63 centimeters) of rain that year, almost twice the yearly average.

There are a number of causes of floods of this kind:

- Deep snowfalls that melt quickly and run off.
- Dams that break.
- Hurricanes that may push high storm waves across a beach and cause a flood on the land.
- Undersea quakes that can cause tsunami waves to flood the land.
- Heavy rainfalls, perhaps the most damaging of all.

A flood such as the one in Southern California begins with a long period of fairly steady rain. At first, the rain soaks into the land and is absorbed by the soil. As it continues, some of the water seeps into the streams. And after the soil gets saturated, additional rain runs across the surface of the ground, downhill, and into the rivers and streams.

Land at the foot of mountain ranges, such as the Los Angeles Basin, is especially susceptible to flooding. High in the mountains, the small streams move quickly and cut deep-sided, V-shaped valleys. The channels of water stay straight and turn only when they hit a large mass of rock that cannot be cut through.

A landslide covers one side of the Pomona Freeway just east of Los Angeles. The hillside was loosened by heavy rains during the winter of 1968–69.

As this water moves down the mountain, other streams join it and eventually a river is formed. This river runs over flatter land than do the mountain streams. As a result, it does not move very fast and has time to carve a winding path across the broad plain. More and more water is added to the other streams. The big river grows deeper and finally spills over its natural banks, spreading quickly across the flat areas on both sides of the channel. This fast-moving water carries with it particles of soil that have washed down from the hillside. As it slows down, the soil is dumped onto the flood plains.

Floods vary greatly in size. Sometimes they cover a few acres and other times they drown millions of acres of farmland and towns. No part of the earth is entirely safe except the highest land.

Dr. Martin Stout, associate professor of geology at California State College, Los Angeles, and a leading engineering geologist, says, "The Southern California environment is hostile and tricky, and it has been ever since the coast rose from the sea."

Violent floods, landslides, erosion, and the brush fires that cause them are all natural processes that result from the unusual rain patterns that are present in Southern California. There is either too much rain or too little.

The summer before the 1969 flood, for example, thick chaparral plants on the hills and in the mountains dried into sticks. During the following dry, hot months, about 100,000 acres (405,000 hectares) of this explosive brush burned wildly. This fire set the foundation for the damage that was to come in January and February.

"Flood follows fire" is a well-known rule of thumb to Southern Californians. Once a brush fire has cleaned off a hill, the ground loses its natural capacity to soak up even a normal rainfall. The water charges down the slopes in torrents, tearing them to pieces as it passes.

When the rain began at the end of that summer, meteorologists predicted an average rainfall. But in the middle of January a record-breaking storm rolled in from the Pacific, near Hawaii. Since it was hidden behind a minor weather disturbance, "it caught us napping," admitted the Los Angeles National Forest district ranger.

Meteorologists at the Los Angeles Forecast Office were aware of the storm but were not able to predict its intensity at the start. Once it started, though, they were accurate until the end. Satellite photographs helped.

It was an unusual storm and Los Angeles residents felt its effect for 9 days. The Weather Service measured rainfall never equaled during any like period on record: 13.15 inches (33.5 centimeters) fell in 9 consecutive days at the Los Angeles Civic Center. And for the entire rainy season, 44 inches (111.75 centimeters) fell in 42 days!

The mid-January rains soaked the normally dry sloping layers that lie beneath the earth's crust. Over the centuries, sliding movements that are typical of earthquake zones cause these layers of clay and other slippery material to tilt and break into pieces. And the weight of the water on the upper soil during that rainy period probably helped loosen their hold. These conditions, added to the February storm, made flooding a certainty.

As the torrential rains came, rivers clogged with debris rampaged off their courses. Then landslides followed the flooding. The surface mud and gravel, already soaked, began to wash down the slopes immediately, smashing hillside homes and pouring through doors and windows.

Some people were trapped in their beds. Little children

in two areas met death this way. An avalanche of mud suffocated two youngsters in Highland Park while they slept. And in Topanga Canyon, a mother and her two children died when a mudslide hit their home.

The pelting rain caused flash floods in many sections, particularly on the hillsides. One group of campers drowned before it could reach safety.

These sudden bursts of water occur when a storm cloud unloads its store of water in one great dumping action. Usually they come from a high-intensity thunderstorm that is short and swift. Strong updrafts in thunderstorms support large drops of water. This allows great amounts of water to accumulate within the thunderstorm cloud. When the storm reaches a certain stage of development, these drops fall to the ground and may result in heavy rainfall in a small area. If this downpour falls in a narrow stream bed, flash flooding may occur.

A thunderstorm results from instability in the atmosphere, which leads to the overturning of layers of air. Two actions that can cause this instability are (1) an intense heating of the layers of the atmosphere near the surface of the earth and (2) a colder air mass moving over the top of a warm air mass.

In the mountains such as those surrounding the Los Angeles Basin, the warm, moist air is usually forced up and over a mountain. As this moisture-heavy air rises, it expands and cools. The cooling leads to condensation. If the air is unstable, then very intense rainfall can result.

Although meteorologists can predict and warn residents of the stages of a seasonal flood, it is not as easy with a flash flood. However, the Weather Service is always on the watch for conditions that lead to flash floods, and it gets the informa-

Two children are rescued after their home was cut off and threatened by flood waters in the Topanga Canyon area.

tion to the public in the fastest way possible. Warning signs are also posted in areas that are subject to flash flooding, such as mountains, gulleys, and valleys. People are advised to stay away from these sites, particularly during the flash flood season.

One of the cities hardest hit by the 1969 flood was Glendora, a beautiful community in the foothills of the San Gabriel Mountains. Many of its 32,050 residents who owned fashionable houses on the winding slopes and canyons of the mountain range saw everything they possessed washed away in a torrent of mud and water. Fortunately, no one in that city died in the flood, but 160 homes were badly damaged and 5 were totally destroyed. Lorin Rimer and his wife were among those hardest hit.

Mr. and Mrs. Rimer came to Southern California in 1947 from Pennsylvania. They bought a house on a nice hillside in Glendora. Then in 1968, during the summer, the slopes behind their home burned, for the first time in half a century, they were told.

When the neighborhood realized the danger, families held a meeting and stocked up on shovels, sandbags and other supplies. "The first heavy rain came on Sunday, January 19," said Mr. Rimer. "On Monday so much mud and water was coming out of the canyon into the street that many of us stayed home to sandbag and shovel muck."

By Tuesday they had a real battle with the coarse gravel and boulders that were hurtling down the mountainside. The neighbors fought them all day and half way into the night.

"Early Wednesday, a cloud burst woke us up," said Mr. Rimer. "By the time I reached the window, the lawn was gone. A neighbor was clinging to the low eaves of our house. The current ripped off his boots, but he made it to high ground."

At that point their house was an island. A window gave way and let in a wall of water and gravel. They realized that muck would be up to the ceiling in a few minutes. The front door was blocked, so Mr. Rimer told his wife to get out through a window. But when she touched the sill, she was knocked back inside. A short circuit in the house wiring had charged the metal window frame.

"I can't do it," she shouted.

"You'll have to," Mr. Rimer called. "Otherwise we'll be buried alive."

On the third try, Mrs. Rimer went out, and Mr. Rimer followed. The water swept them about 100 yards (about 90 meters) before they could crawl to a house on a high lawn. Mr. Rimer tried to stand up but discovered that his pajamas were filled with heavy gravel. His legs were cut and bleeding, but the couple was safe.

In many areas where hillside homes were anchored to the slopes by stilts, the flood sent them down the slippery soil like so many toys.

In the Santa Monica Mountains, Twentieth Century-Fox's film set for *Planet of the Apes* was turned into a twisted heap of rubble.

Coastal towns such as Ventura, Santa Barbara, and Carpinteria also took a severe beating from the mud and water. Wharves were wrecked beyond repair, and a hundred boats were buried or swept out to sea.

Citrus groves were destroyed in Ventura, Santa Barbara, and San Luis Obispo counties, causing a loss of $30 million worth of oranges, lemons, flowers, sugar beets, and vegetables.

The Los Angeles County Flood Control District, established in 1915, has worked long and hard to predict and prevent flooding, but its task never ends. As more and more people move to Southern California, more protection is required.

The Santa Clara River, for example, had been flooding for many years. But until the population increased in that area, it didn't cause much damage.

"The big problem is building adequate defenses before more people arrive and get clobbered," said Brigadier General William M. Glasgow of the U.S. Army Corps of Engineers.

Earth scientists have helped a great deal in this area. Geologists inspect and map the deep layers of the earth. And they use air photos, which often show things that can't be seen from the ground.

Scientists continue to study the earth and atmosphere so they can improve people's chances for safety from floods and mud slides. But there is still a great deal to learn. In the meantime, building codes have been changed. One of the most important rules states that no one may construct a building or home on a dangerously steep slope, in an area that is known to be unstable, or on hills which are made of *fill*. *Fill* is soil that is not compacted enough to form a solid base for constructing buildings.

This decision, however, and other measures to prevent damage, were of little help during the months following the 1969 flood. One hundred people had died—drowned or were buried—in their homes from the waves of mud, or in storm-related accidents. Property damage was estimated at $1 billion, and insurance covered almost none of it.

Southern California, however, continues to be a favorite spot for thousands of visitors and residents. In spite of the threat of water, mud, and the trembling earth beneath it, people still flock to its mountains, forests, and shores—the land of fun in the sun!

CHAPTER FIVE

GREAT HURRICANE CAMILLE (1969)

While the people of Gulfport, Mississippi, enjoyed the last of the summer season, a huge storm thousands of miles away began to brew. Slowly the band of clouds drifted westward from Dakar, West Africa, toward the Gulf of Mexico. It had started as a long, narrow area of low pressure first sighted on a weather satellite photograph taken on August 5, 1969.

On the morning of August 14, a Navy Hurricane Hunter plane flew through the storm, reporting winds of 60 miles (96 kilometers) per hour. "Hurricane hunters" fly reconnaissance planes for the National Weather Service. Their job is to spot and track brewing storms from the air. They even fly over and through the storms to find out how strong they are.

Hurricanes are also detected by high-altitude camera-carrying balloons, by coastal radar networks, and by high-speed electronic data computers. All of these means help the National Weather Service to gather and evaluate the information it needs to issue warnings of approaching hurricanes.

It is almost impossible to track them with complete accuracy, though, because these storms often change their pattern unexpectedly. This was the case with Hurricane Camille. By August 15, its winds had increased to more than 75 mph (120 kph).

Because it was the third hurricane of that season, the National Weather Service (at that time called the U.S. Weather Bureau) named it Camille, following a custom begun in 1953. Every season since 1953, the service has used a list of women's names in alphabetical order. As each hurricane appears, it receives a name like Alma, Beulah, Connie, Diane, Edna, and so on. Each is then tracked by its given name until it breaks up at sea or over land. (In 1978 it was announced that hurricanes would also be given men's names.)

For two days, Hurricane Camille hung over the Gulf of

Mexico. It seemed undecided about its next move. First, it drifted toward the Florida panhandle. At one point, it appeared to move westward. Finally, it gathered enough strength and began churning quickly toward the Mississippi Gulf Coast.

For days the Weather Service had issued warnings about the hurricane. Two square red and black hurricane flags were hoisted, predicting the force of the winds. Some people paid attention to the reports. Others ignored them.

Residents along the coast had only twelve hours to decide whether to stay or leave. More than 50,000 fled inland to Hattiesburg and Jackson.

In the resort community of Pass Christian, Mississippi, 6,000 people had packed the beach during the hot mid-August days. But time for relaxation and enjoyment was running out. Pass Christian was directly in the path of Hurricane Camille.

Police Chief Jerry Peralta drove along the beach highway, U.S. 90, knocking on doors and urging every person he saw to leave. Three thousand visitors and residents escaped as the hurricane approached, but the rest stayed behind seeking the highest available ground, about 20 feet (about 6 meters) above sea level.

When Peralta stopped at the Richelieu Apartments overlooking the beach, twenty people at a party there refused to move, assuming they would be safe on the second floor of the building. But it was a foolish decision.

Within a few hours, a rolling wave as high as a three-story building crashed over the seawall. The Richelieu Apartments were overwhelmed as the wild wind and water tore the structure to pieces. People were carried off screaming in a terrifying 20-foot (6-meter) tide.

For more than four hours, Hurricane Camille continued to tear Pass Christian to shreds. Winds of 190 mph (305

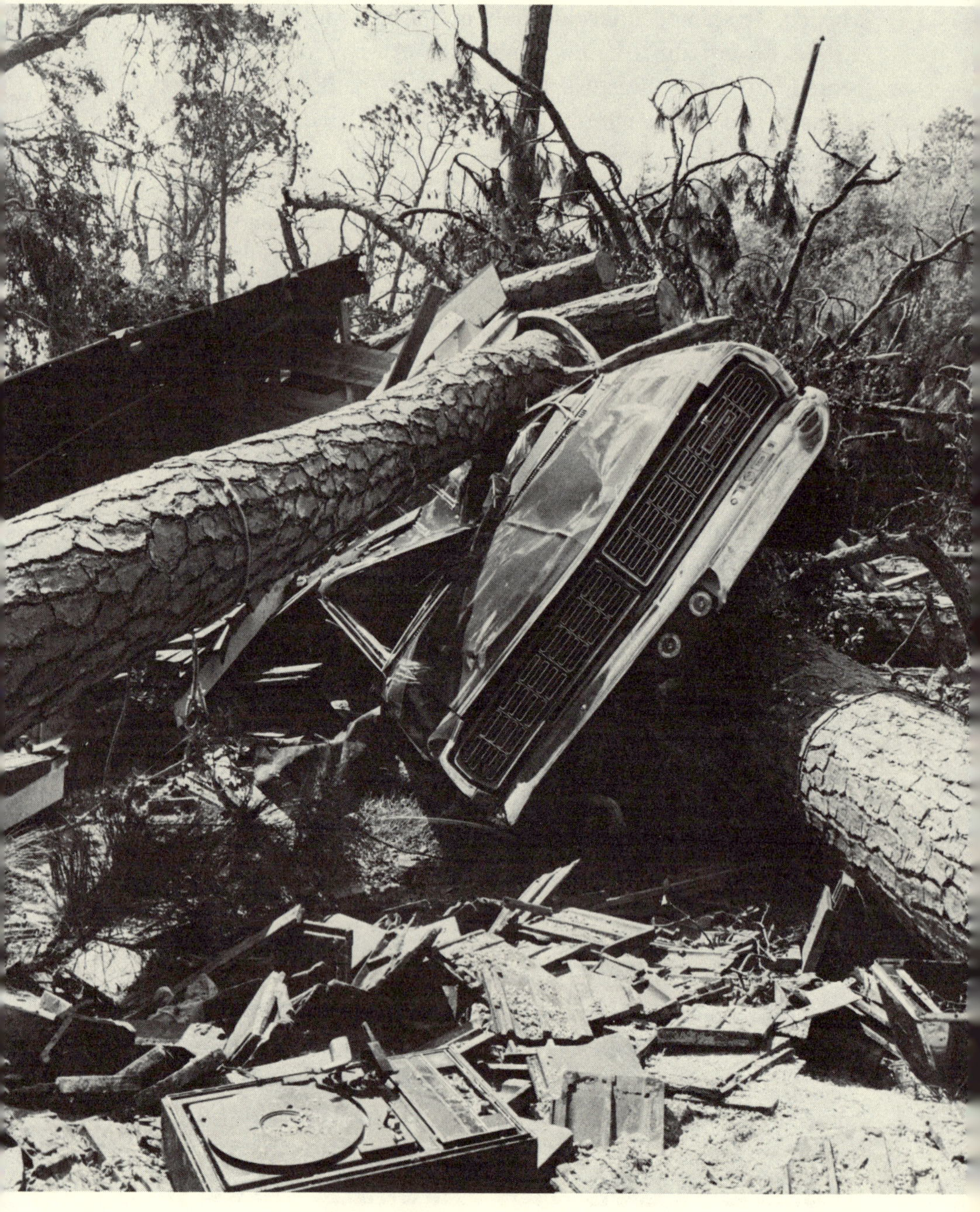

kph) ripped everything apart. More than 125 people died in this community alone. And the damage was beyond belief.

"The wind sound changed," said a summer visitor, Tom Perrin. "I never heard anything like that. It felt like fifteen or twenty tornadoes had caught us. There wasn't any way to get ready for them. If you got low, you'd drown. If you stayed high, the tornado or the hurricane would pick you right up. There wasn't anything at all to do."

Camille was not an ordinary storm. Hundreds of citizens suffered serious injuries. And scores of homes collapsed. In Gulfport-Biloxi, Mississippi, alone, 2,000 homes were destroyed and 2,000 more were damaged.

Afterward, Highway 90 was piled so high at one point with furniture, boats, fragments of buildings, and other debris, that it took two years to repair the damage fully.

Before the storm, 114 fashionable homes graced the beachfront area of Gulfport. After the storm, only 6 had escaped major damage. And 9 houses completely disappeared.

One family and several of their friends decided to ride out the storm in their home. But they might have changed their minds if they could have known what was ahead. Mrs. Sharon Wells and her two children were among them.

To prepare for the hurricane, everyone pitched in, including the youngest children. They kept their radios tuned to news of Camille. Carefully, they cleaned and filled the bathtub with water for use during and after the storm, in case the regular supply became polluted. They also filled pots and bottles with drinking water and put flashlights in easily seen

A demolished car lies among the debris left by Hurricane Camille in August 1969.

places. Patio furniture, bicycles, garbage cans, and other outdoor equipment were carried inside.

But nothing could have prepared the families for Camille's brutal attack. Even before the wind reached its highest speed, the house began to shudder and creak.

Wind-driven rain blasted the house and soaked through the thick walls. Rain flooded in as the front door blew off. The ceiling gave way next, and huge pieces of plaster fell to the floor.

The hurricane winds, both positive (those forces pushing in) and negative (those forces pulling out) blew the house apart as if it were made of twigs. The winds of 200 mph (320 kph) exerted more than a ton of pressure on each 10 square feet (1 square meter) of the windward side of the building. After the front door blew off, the house was wrenched from its foundation. Another great gust tore the roof from the structure.

"We'd be in a room and it would start falling apart," said Mrs. Wells. "We'd just get out when it would fall in. The water was up to my shoulders, so I just grabbed the kids."

The shaking group huddled together in one small room of the second floor. Around them, two walls had caved in, but luckily the floor continued to hold them. All fifteen were saved.

A few hours after midnight on August 18, the worst was over in the Gulfport area. As the winds died down, Chief Peralta began wading through chest-high water toward St. Paul's School in Pass Christian, where 450 refugees were gathered for food and shelter.

With the help of two National Guard amphibious Ducks, he began rescuing survivors. "I guess we found fifty people that first trip," he recalled. "They were hanging in trees and just screaming and crying. At the school, the people inside were holding their babies over their heads. It was all over and the wind had stopped and the tide was going down, but they were just standing there and screaming, holding their kids up."

At 9:00 A.M., Peralta tried out the short-wave radio in the fire truck, and it got them through to the outside for the first time. Before long, bulldozers and trucks driven by Marine reservists appeared with medical supplies, drinking water, and old clothes.

Those who survived recounted their frightening experiences. One elderly woman had been thrown out of her house when it was torn from its foundation. She landed in a large bush and hung on until the storm was over.

A motel was wrecked and buried under tons of fish fertilizer blown from more than half a mile away. An automobile stood on its front wheels with its back wheels balanced on a tree trunk.

One boat was blown halfway through a house, and another landed in a parking lot three blocks from the beach. Oceangoing ships weighing thousands of tons were tossed onto the shore like so many toy boats.

An entire orange crop was wiped out in Plaquemines Parish, Louisiana. And hundreds of shrimp boats and other small craft were destroyed by the storm.

Railroad station buildings and equipment along a 35-mile (56-kilometer) stretch from Wiggins, Mississippi, to Gulfport also suffered extensive damage.

"Evil spirits and big winds" is the way the Caribbean Indians referred to these storms that sweep out of the Gulf of Mexico, the Caribbean, and the warm, sunny part of the Atlantic Ocean. The word *hurricane* comes from the Spanish *huracán*, derived from the name of the Mayan storm god, *Hunraken*.

When these storms originate in other oceans and a different hemisphere, they are called by different names. For

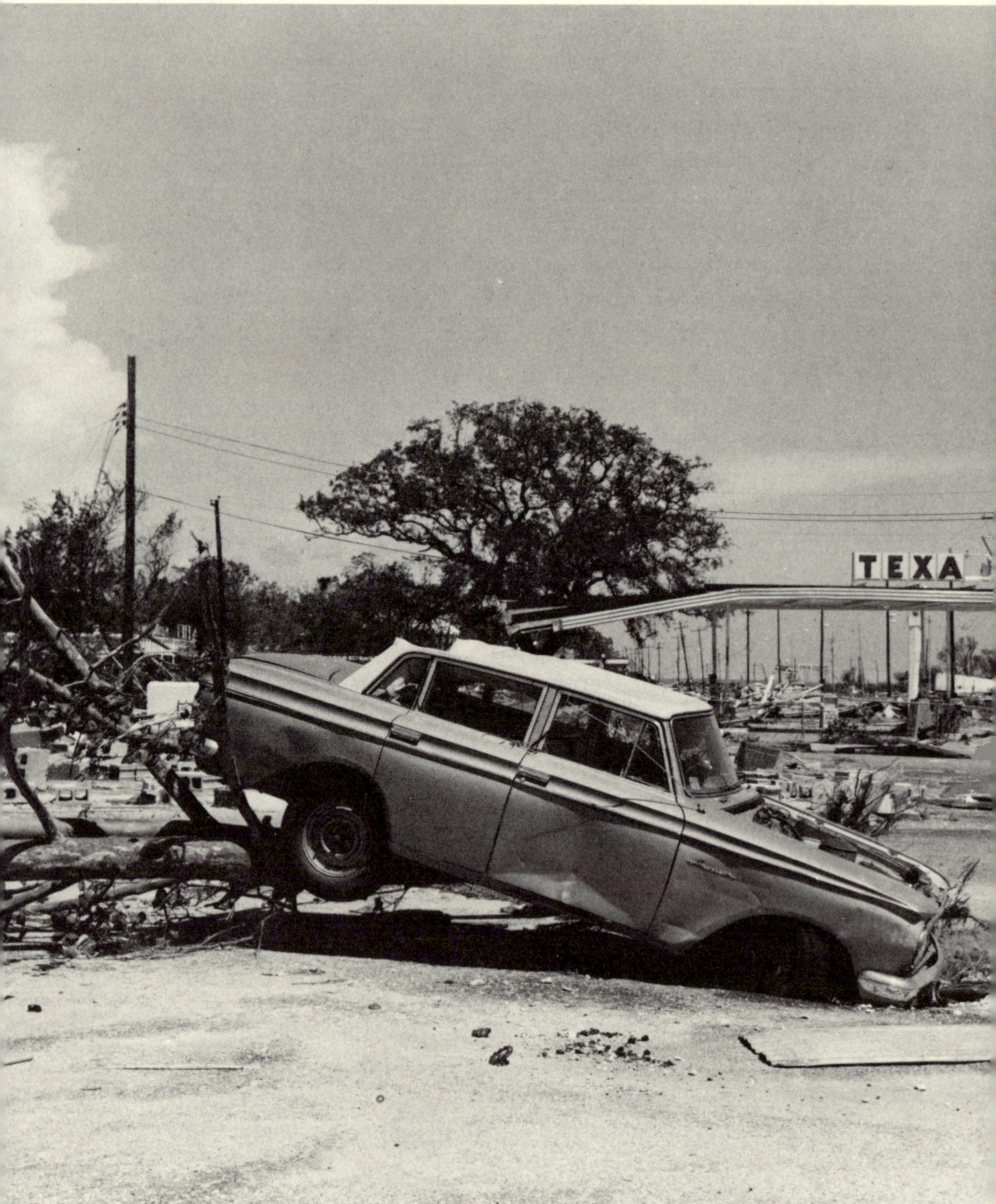
TEXA

example, in the Philippine Islands, such a storm is known as *baguio*. In the Indian Ocean, it is referred to as a *cyclone*. And in the Pacific, from the Philippine Islands to Japan and along the coast of China, it is often called a *typhoon*. But whatever the name, the intensity of these storms and their power to destroy are the same.

Hurricanes and typhoons begin quietly enough. At the start, they're simply disturbances of gently whirling winds with a slight lowering of pressure. The rotating earth gives them their counterclockwise movement in the Northern Hemisphere and their clockwise motion in the Southern Hemisphere.

These storms usually move up from the tropics, often heading for the southern coasts of the United States, in late summer or early fall, as did Hurricane Camille. And they are generally accompanied by heavy rains, high waves, and high tides.

The destructive whirlpools revolve around a central area of extreme low pressure, originally named by sailors "the eye of the storm." Inside the *eye* is an eerie calm where there is almost no wind and no rain and the sun shines in a clear sky. The measurement across the eye is usually between 5 and 25 miles (between 8 and 40 kilometers). The real danger is outside the eye. Circling around it are intense, furious winds that often reach 100 to 200 mph (160 to 320 kph).

Hurricanes form over warm tropical oceans, usually 10° to 20° north or south of the equator. This location is a zone of maximum heating of the earth's surface and also one where the lower layers of the atmosphere become quite moist.

A car and gas station are among the wreckage left by Hurricane Camille.

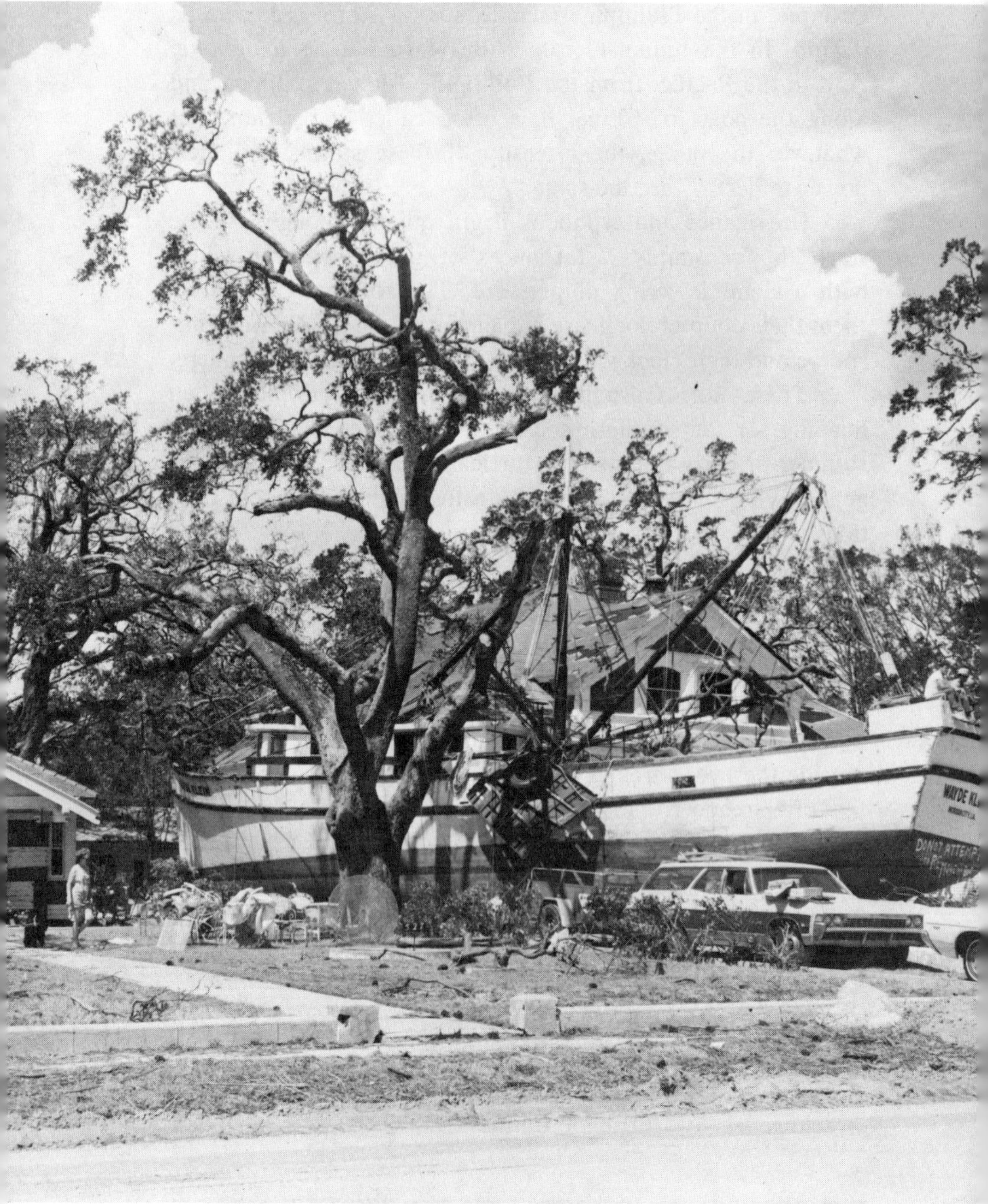

Meteorologists say this combination of strong heating and high moisture content makes the air unstable. Unstable air overturns easily, and this produces updrafts and downdrafts.

In regions of strong updrafts, cumulus clouds form and may grow into cumulonimbus, or rain clouds. Sometimes the clouds take on a cyclonic rotation when they develop in a region where the winds converge or meet. One such convergence zone exists along the dividing line between the northeast trades and the southeast trades.

If the showers that result become strong enough and concentrated enough, the pressure gets lower and *cyclonic flow* develops. A tropical cyclone is then born. When the cyclone reaches a minimum of 74 mph (119 kph), it is called a *hurricane*.

The heavy rains that result from a hurricane rapidly release the stored-up heat caused by the condensation of moisture. This may be one source of the hurricane's violent energy. Trade winds from the east carry the storm toward the west. A hurricane has its greatest strength over the ocean. If its track pulls it over the land, it weakens. This is due to a loss of heat and because the supply of water vapor from the ocean's surface is cut off.

Hurricanes that follow a "regular track"—along their C-shaped path—tend to curve back out into the Atlantic Ocean near Cape Hatteras, North Carolina, where they "blow themselves out" at sea.

A fishing trawler was driven ashore by Hurricane Camille in August 1969.

On August 19, Hurricane Camille was thought to be *dead*. During the next few hours, however, it moved slowly over Tennessee and Kentucky, dropping a moderate amount of rain. And when it crossed the Appalachian Mountains, it joined forces with a rainfall that had moved into Virginia from the northwest. That night, 31 inches (79 centimeters) of rain fell within a few hours. Scientists claim that this amount of rain, on the average, occurs only once in a thousand years.

Landslides followed the heavy flooding. Rivers overflowed, carrying tons of rock and dirt over towns and farmland. In one area, 155 people were killed, most of them victims of the floodwaters. At one time, the James River in Richmond, Virginia, carried 222,000 cubic feet (6,280 cubic meters) of water past the capital city each second.

The village of Tyro, Virginia, was particularly affected. While a mother, father, and their two teen-age daughters slept, their house was torn from its foundation. Everyone was washed from the house as it rolled over and over. A huge wave threw the youngest girl into a tree, where she clung for seventeen hours. Later, the rest of her family was found dead.

In another house, parents grabbed their two small children as the water rose slowly in the rooms. When the bed where they sat floated to the ceiling, the whole house flew apart. The children were torn from their parents' arms and carried off in a muddy wave of water. Only the mother and father survived.

After three days over land, August 17–20, Camille headed back to sea near Norfolk, Virginia. The winds weakened after so much overland travel, but they still averaged 65 to 70 mph (105 to 113 kph). By August 22, there remained only traces of the hurricane—the most intense storm ever to strike the United States.

More than 250 people were killed as a result of the hurricane and flood, and damage to property reached nearly $1.5 billion. President Nixon declared the coastal areas of Alabama, Mississippi, and Louisiana disaster zones. And Virginia and West Virginia requested—and received—the same official status, which made them eligible for federal funds. The disaster areas eventually received roughly $350 million in federal aid.

Most people were in a state of shock for a long time following the disaster. Many simply stood by the smashed remains of their homes and wept over lost family and friends. They weren't sure how to begin living again.

Refugee centers were packed. The Red Cross, the Salvation Army, and the Mennonite Disaster Service offered a great deal of help. The Mennonites alone donated 20,000 man-days to their refugee neighbors. The federal government sent 800,000 pounds (360,000 kilograms) of food.

By the following spring, most of the areas were on the way to recovery. Those who survived will never forget Camille, nor will they forget the support and friendship they found in each other.

Mayor J. J. Wittmann of Pass Christian, Mississippi, seemed to express everyone's disbelief as he watched victims dig their way out of the disaster. "Most of these people have been through hurricanes before," he said. "We had no reason to expect that this one would be so bad."

It was not likely that residents would ever take another hurricane warning lightly.

CHAPTER SIX

TORNADO ALLEY (1974)

In Brandenburg, Kentucky, 32 miles (51 kilometers) west of Louisville, Leck Craycroft and his mother-in-law returned home from shopping. It was Wednesday, April 3, 1974. As they put the grocery bags on the kitchen table, a sudden train-like noise roared overhead. Quickly, Leck pulled his mother-in-law toward the basement. When they were halfway down the stairs, the house blew apart.

Within minutes, a raging tornado had swooped down on the quiet town of 1,700 and torn apart nearly half the homes and businesses.

The furious wind funnel, with speeds between 100 and 300 mph (160 to 480 kph), dragged Craycroft along the ground like a pull-toy. Bruised and bleeding, he fell to the ground 100 yards (90 meters) from his house. Through the pelting rain, he could see that Green Street was gone. The familiar neighborhood houses, trees, lawns, cars, and utility poles had all disappeared.

There was nothing left of his home but the hole where the basement had been. The tornado had torn away the basement cinder-block walls and had even stolen the steel posts from the concrete floor. His car was a heap of crushed metal. And his mother-in-law lay dead under a pile of debris.

As he ran down the street to his wife's office, children and adults walked by him in a daze. He found Mrs. Craycroft safe in the basement of the Rural Electric Cooperative Corporation, where she worked.

"Ona, your mom's gone," he said. "I held on to her as long as I could. She's gone. Everything's gone!"

But the tragedy wasn't over for the Craycrofts. In the street in front of Alta Dugan's Beauty Salon, Leck's sister-in-law, Eleanor Craycroft, lay dead. She had just finished a hair appointment.

The tornado in Brandenburg killed twenty-nine people,

mostly children caught playing outside after school. This devastating tornado was just one of more than one hundred that erupted that day in the South, East, and Midwest from widespread storms. The other vicious whirlpools ripped through an area known as "Tornado Alley," including sections of Tennessee, Georgia, Alabama, Virginia, West Virginia, North Carolina, Illinois, Indiana, Ohio; and Michigan. This region is a natural meeting place for the cool air masses that come from the north and the warm air masses that come from the south—conditions that usually trigger a tornado.

These small, severe storms form several thousand feet above the surface of the earth, usually during warm, humid, unsettled weather and often with a heavy thunderstorm. Sometimes two or more tornadoes spring from the same thunderstorm. As the thunderstorm moves, as on the day of the hundred tornadoes in 1974, tornadoes form at different places along its path. They generally travel for a few miles and then break up. The forward speed of a tornado can range from almost no motion to as much as 70 mph (113 kph).

Hailstones as large as golf balls rained down on parts of Georgia that terrifying April day, and battered everything in sight. In Sugar Valley, neighbors found the Goble house completely shattered. Nine-year-old Randall Goble, hysterical, ran in circles near the ruins.

After the frightened boy was taken to the Gordon County Hospital, he cried to a nurse, "Tell me it was a bad dream. Where's my mommy and daddy?"

The answer was more than a bad dream. His parents and two sisters were later found dead in the den of their flattened house. Randall survived because the tornado's winds had picked him up and carried him 200 yards (180 meters) before throwing him to the ground.

At Monticello, Indiana, a tornado leveled most of the

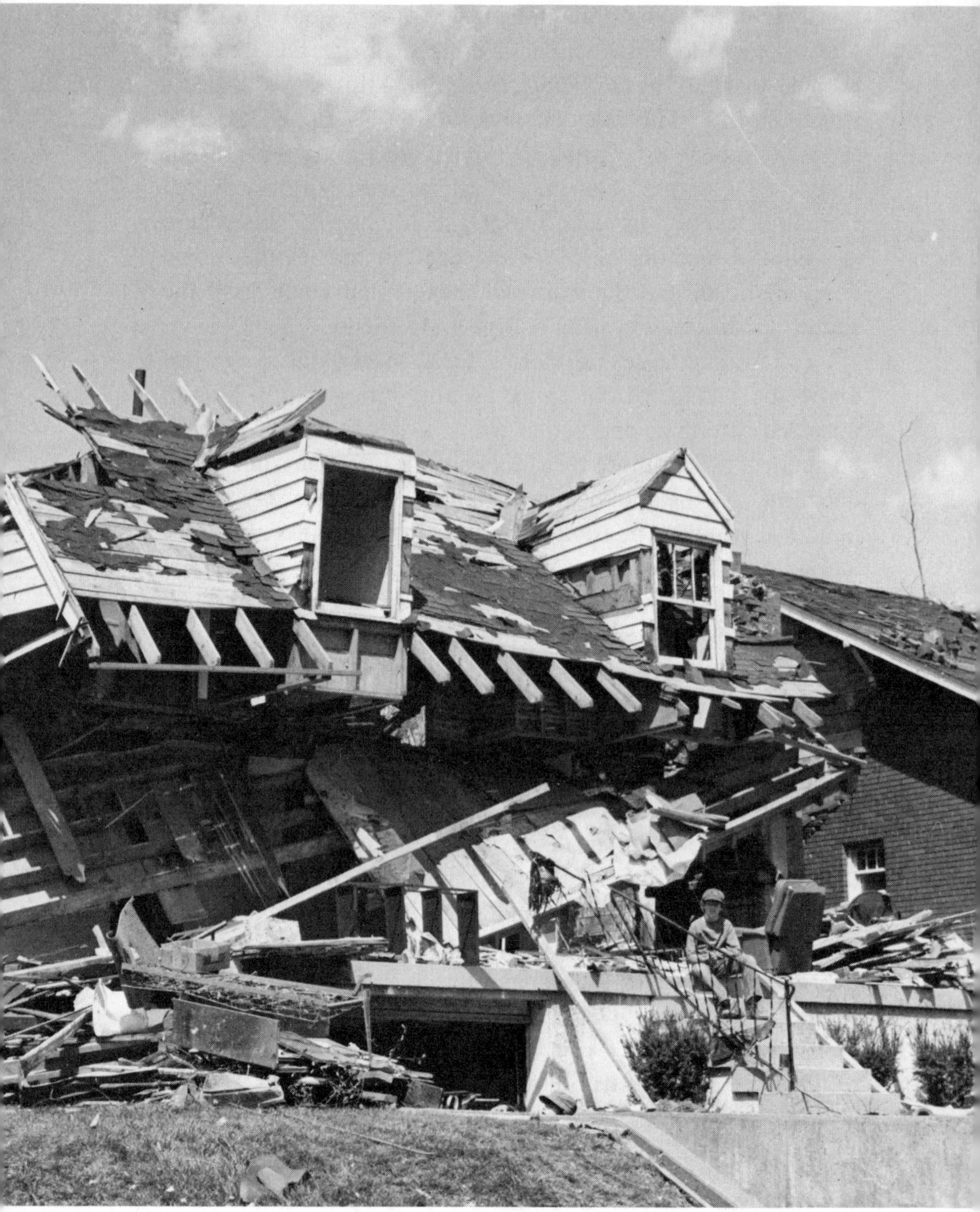

business district before it roared down Lake Freeman. There it lifted four sections of the Penn Central railroad building off concrete pilings, blew them 40 feet (12.5 meters) through the air, and dumped them into the lake. Each section weighed 115 tons (104 metric tons).

Xenia, Ohio, was next. Six of the town's twelve schools, five supermarkets, and hundreds of homes were ravaged. "We had about thirty seconds' warning before it hit," said Gary Heflin, a grocery-store manager. "All you could hear was the wind, the crashes, and the people praying."

Those who had been tuned to their radios and televisions received about fifteen minutes' warning. And anyone who looked to the southwest could see the deadly black cloud approaching, ready to pounce on the city of 27,000.

Many residents acted quickly. They remembered to open a few windows to ease the imbalance of pressure inside and outside the buildings. Some fled to their basements for shelter. And others in houses, schools, and shopping centers without basements crouched in hallways, closets, and bathrooms.

Nearly half the city was destroyed, leaving 34 people dead, and more than 1,600 injured. But within an hour, the survivors began to function again. They fought their way out of the rubble and started looking for lost family and friends.

Despite the widespread damage to eleven states and part of Canada, the April 3 tornadoes did not come as a complete

A tornado-damaged home in Louisville, Kentucky. Following the April 1974 tornadoes, 7,000 families were given emergency assistance in the Kentucky area alone.

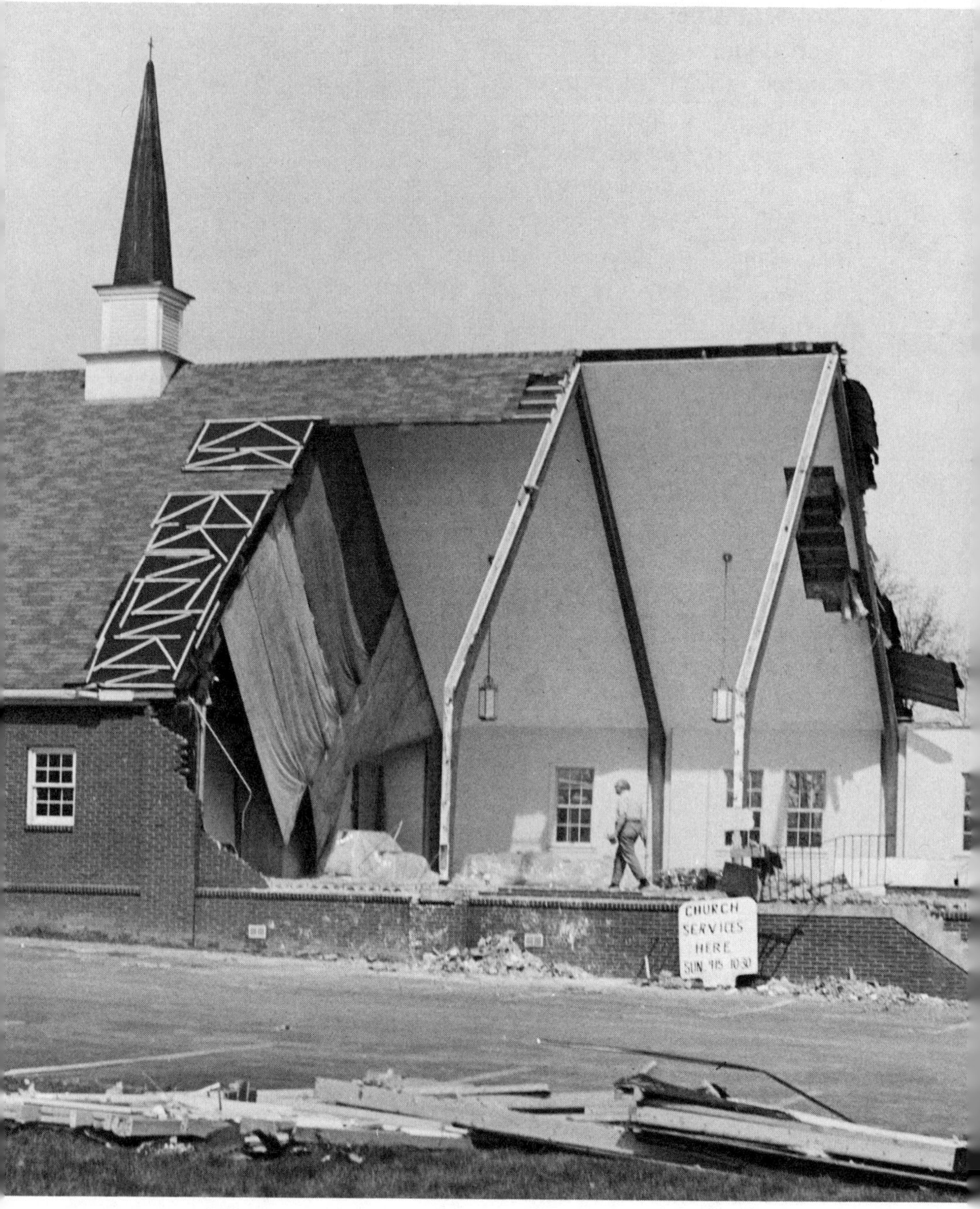
CHURCH
SERVICES
HERE
SUN. 9:15 10:30

surprise. In Kansas City the day before, meteorologists at the Severe Storms Forecast Center noticed that a low-pressure system with cool air behind it was forming over the Central States, between the Rocky Mountains and the Appalachians.

At the National Weather Service Station in Louisville, Kentucky, the teleprinter tapped out a warning:

> TORNADOES REPORTED NEAR HARDINSBURG AND THREE MILES [FIVE KILOMETERS] NORTHWEST OF IRVINGTON AROUND 3:45 P.M. MOVING NORTHEAST ABOUT 50 MPH [80 KPH]. THE TORNADO WARNING IS IN EFFECT.

It was a message listeners were not likely to ignore because there is no other storm quite like the tornado. Because of the dark, swirling thunderstorm clouds from which it springs, the tornado is especially frightening. It is different from any other storm. A long, winding, funnel-shaped cloud dangles toward the earth from the black storm clouds above it. A tornado (sometimes called a *twister*) is actually a whirlpool (vortex) of wind spinning like a top, in a counterclockwise direction, at tremendous speed. It can sometimes reach 300 mph (480 kph) or more.

At times, the swirling mass will simply dangle and not touch the ground; but if it does meet the earth, destruction begins. Wreckage flies in all directions. It can destroy solid buildings in seconds, uproot large trees, hurl people and animals for hundreds of yards, and toss ships and railroad cars as though they were toys.

Despite tornado damage, Sunday worshipers attended services in the basement of this Sayler Park, Ohio, church.

A school bus was tossed 490 feet (150 m) into a housing area by the tornado that hit Xenia, Ohio, in April of 1974.

75

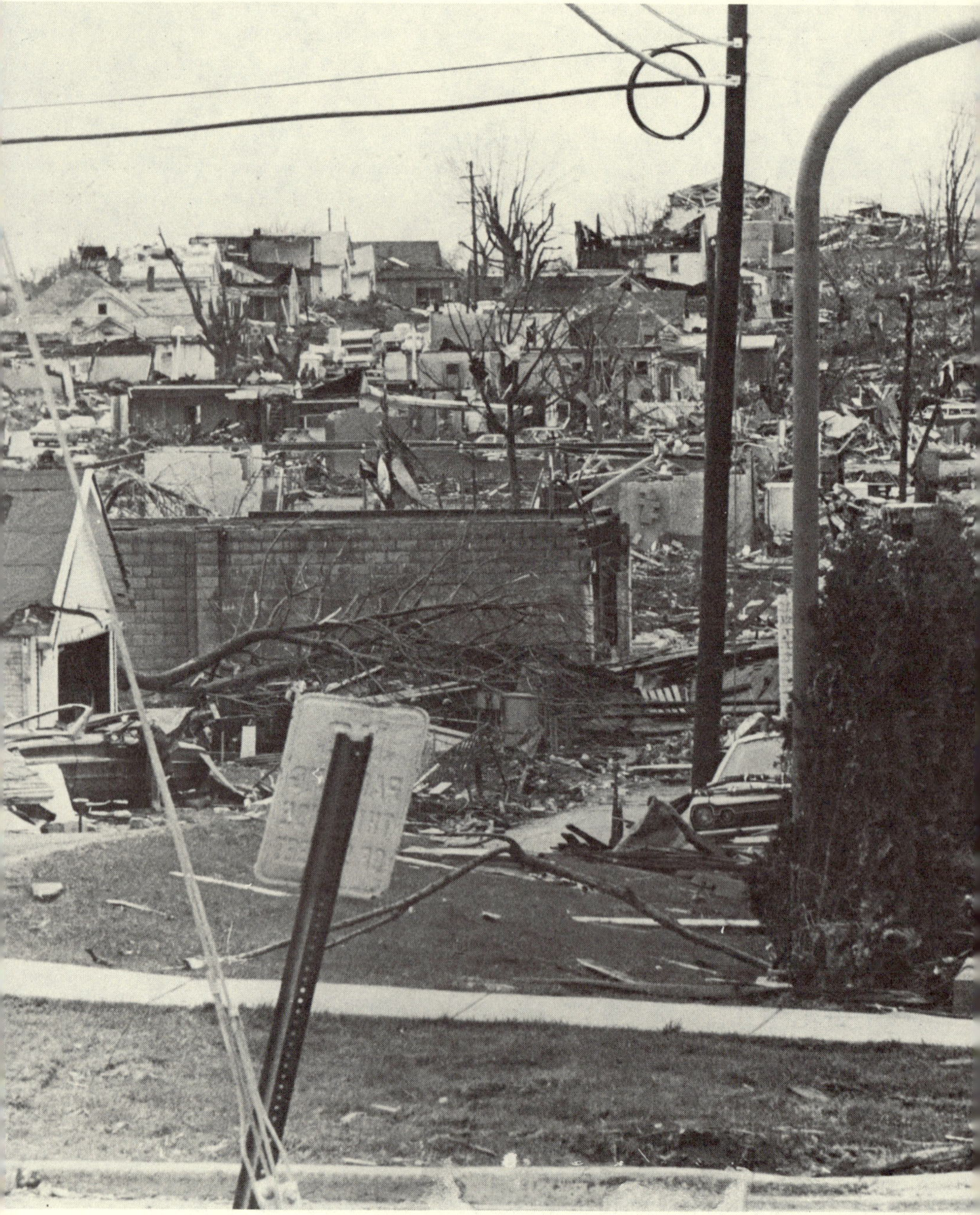

Not even the most stable steel and concrete structures are able to remain standing. The funnel acts something like a vacuum cleaner because of the upward-rushing air (*centrifucal force*) produced by its rapidly spinning winds. A tornado can pick up a house or truck like a speck of dust on a carpet.

Occasionally, a tornado teases an area by dipping and rising over a long stretch of land. The result is a checkerboard of touched and untouched squares. Where it reaches the ground, objects are whirled upward. In Hanover, Indiana, for example, a twister picked up a house, turned it around, then set it down without harming anyone inside. With the earth's dust, the tornado takes on an eerie, black appearance. And to some it has the sound of a roaring train or a thousand exploding cannons.

Tornadoes don't just blow buildings down like hurricanes. They also *explode* them. Surrounding air usually presses against the structure with a force of about 15 pounds on every square inch (1 kilogram per square centimeter). At the same time, the air inside the house presses out just as hard.

As long as the air is not disturbed, the inside and outside pressure is balanced. But when a tornado passes over a house, the outside air is sucked away. Inside air, however, still pushes out against the walls. Since there is a great deal less pressure pushing back from the outside, the walls are then pushed out in a explosion. The house is blown to bits.

Three forces cause the widespread damage associated with tornadoes:

A residential area in Xenia hit by the April 1974 tornado.

- High winds
- Expansion of buildings due to pressure imbalance
- Lifting effect of the violent upward winds

In Bear Branch, Indiana, the Halbert Walston family experienced the effects of these powerful forces firsthand.

Mr. Walston looked out a window and saw the ugly black swirl approaching. He yelled to his children and his wife, Alice. "Everybody into the bathroom!"

Mrs. Walston and their four children made it into the bathroom, but as Mr. Walston made a flying leap to get through the door, he was blasted out the bathroom wall. Next, his family was blown into the backyard.

Walston was in the air for about 40 feet (12 meters). As he fell to the ground, he saw his five-year-old daughter, Amy, fly over an apple tree about 75 feet (23 meters) from the house. The wind carried her gently to earth, then dropped a piece of tin on top of her.

Mrs. Walston staggered to her feet, cut and bleeding. Her face began to swell. She found her little daughter whimpering under the tin. Sixteen-year-old Bonetta suffered a brain concussion, and Dolly, thirteen, sat silently in a daze. Michael, fifteen, stared at the sky. His arm hung, partially severed at the elbow, and his nose was smashed.

Mr. Walston had a broken ankle and five broken ribs, a punctured lung, and one arm badly cut and bleeding. But he rolled over and crawled slowly to his son. He then pressed his thumb against the boy's artery to stop the bleeding.

Mrs. Walston picked up Amy and, with her two older daughters, started down the road to find help. Mr. Walston kept his thumb in place for an hour until rescuers came. He saved his son's life.

One of the hardest-hit regions was northwestern Alabama. Jasper, a city of 11,300, was almost wiped out. Damages ran to $14 million. Radio announcer Joel Cook of station WARF was nearly speechless in reporting the disaster. "We can't talk to the police department," he gasped, "it just blew away."

In all, more than 300 lives were lost, and property damage was estimated at nearly $600 million for towns from Alabama to Canada. President Nixon declared Alabama, Kentucky, Ohio, Indiana, Georgia, West Virginia, Illinois, North Carolina, Michigan, and Tennessee disaster areas.

Federal, private, and church rescue and relief agencies moved in immediately, providing food, clothing, and shelter. Trucks and bulldozers began inching their way through the streets of rubble, fallen trees, and demolished buildings. The Federal Disaster Assistance Administration coordinated the expenditure of over $100 million by federal agencies.

Although death and destruction were everywhere, a sign of hope soon replaced the despair in people's eyes. From New York to Washington, all across the country, individuals jumped on airplanes and flew in to help their friends and neighbors.

CHAPTER SEVEN

BLIZZARD IN BUFFALO (1977)

A snowflake is one of nature's most exquisite creations. It is formed in the atmosphere by water vapor condensed in below-freezing temperatures. No two snowflakes are exactly alike. Each one takes its unique shape around some minute particle in the air, usually a speck of dust. When it is fully developed, a snowflake is made up of a number of opaque ice crystals.

A fresh snowfall can dress trees, shrubs, mountains, and buildings in a shimmering gown of white. The whiteness comes from the light reflecting off the countless surfaces of the tiny crystals.

But severe layers of snow, sleet, and high, bitter-cold winds can change the same scene into disaster. The atmosphere that covers our earth is usually a stable mass. But when it becomes unbalanced, the resulting weather development may lead to death and destruction.

The condition of the winter atmosphere pretty much determines what the snowflakes will be like when they strike the earth. But it is difficult to believe that such beautiful lacy crystals can, at times, paralyze cities, shut down buildings, suspend classes, and trap travelers on highways.

A heavy blizzard also separates rural people from food, fuel supplies, and medical care. And farmers often lose great numbers of their cattle during a winter storm from hunger, thirst, and cold.

Between January 16, 1977, and February 12, 1977, the citizens of nine counties in upstate New York, and the city of Buffalo, in particular, became victims of one of the worst series of blizzards in the state's history.

The National Weather Service at Greater Buffalo International Airport in Cheektowaga classified the blizzard as *severe*. A severe blizzard is one made up of steady winds of

45 mph (72 kph) or more, a blinding thickness of snow, and temperatures of 10° F (−12° C) or lower.

The Buffalo blizzard broke all records since 1870, when the National Weather Service began keeping records. Wind gusts on January 28 hit a high of 69 mph (110 kph). And on January 29 at 5:00 P.M., the mercury peaked at 1° F above zero (−18° C). From 3:00 to 8:00 A.M., the temperature held at −7° F (−22° C), a record low for the date.

The extreme cold by itself was very uncomfortable and caused great damage. But when the strong wind joined the freezing cold, the combined effect was that of temperatures almost 50° F (almost 28° C) lower. These conditions can chill the human body quickly and lead to such serious consequences as frostbite, lung injury, and even death.

According to the *Buffalo Courier-Express,* twenty-three storm-related deaths were recorded in western New York. And eighteen deaths occurred in Erie county. Eleven of these were in the city of Buffalo.

One young man, Paul Dengler, was rescued from his car half-frozen. "You can't believe what terror it was," he said later. "I watched the needle on the gas gauge slowly dip to 'E,' and then the engine coughed dead."

When a policeman pulled Dengler from his car, his eyebrows and mustache were encrusted in ice, and he was unable to move his arms or legs. But, fortunately, they rescued him in time to save his life.

Fierce winter storms of this type rapidly push across many miles. And they are accompanied by swirling clouds that move in a counterclockwise direction in the Northern Hemisphere.

These cloud masses range over a wide area, sometimes thousands of square miles. They are called *intense low-pres-*

sure systems, and they frequently get their start in the north temperate zone. The trouble spot begins where the polar front and a warm air mass clash over the ocean. One of the starting grounds farthest from the United States is at the extreme western side of the Pacific Ocean, off the coast of Asia.

Another source of winter storms is in the north-central part of the Pacific Ocean. There the frigid Arctic air and the warm air from farther south battle for supremacy.

The storm that results usually rides an eastward-moving wind system that generally breaks up when it hits the Rocky Mountains. But a storm like the Buffalo blizzard is so intense that it manages to hurdle the Rockies and continues on to the Great Lakes region, which is along the storm track of many winter cyclones. These heavy winter storms are frequently accompanied by cold waves, ice or glaze, heavy snow, or a combination of these. Often in a single winter blizzard, the type of precipitation (the quantity of snow or rain) changes several times.

As the fierce winds howled across Lake Erie (one of the Great Lakes), with little warning, in late January 1977, nearly all business and movement in the city of Buffalo and western New York came to a halt. The National Weather Service had issued a blizzard warning, but for many residents it came too late. Ten-foot (3-meter) snowdrifts cut off entire neighborhoods. Others as high as 30 feet (9 meters) buried roads in many areas.

Buffalo's location on a narrow peninsula attracts snow more than most cities' because it catches the moisture-laden winds off Lake Erie so easily. Since the autumn before the blizzard, the city had received an unbelievable 14 feet (4.3 meters) of snow.

Seventeen thousand workers in their downtown offices

were trapped as the blizzard hit the area. And some 5,000 automobiles were left on roadsides when all traffic stopped.

In the suburb of Lancaster, snow piled over the roofs of 66 cars in just one 2-mile (3.2-kilometer) stretch of roadway. Some 400 motorists found shelter in the Liberty Bank Building, where they slept on chairs and floors.

It was the most dramatic weather event in James E. Smith's twenty-five-year career in forecasting. Smith, the meteorologist in charge of the National Weather Service's Buffalo office, referred to the paralyzing winter as "the last straw," and announced his retirement to go into effect the end of February.

During the difficult weekend of January 28–30, Buffalo's 435,000 residents realized the meaning of their town's nickname, "The City of Good Neighbors."

The Statler Hilton Hotel passed out sheets and towels, and crammed four people into some rooms. "Even the lobby was wall-to-wall people," said one hotel employee.

Five hundred patients at the Edward J. Meyer Memorial Hospital crowded closer together so that 2,000 unexpected visitors could find a place to sleep.

Fire departments set up soup and spaghetti lines. And friends and strangers alike shared homes and snowmobiles.

The Salvation Army served meals to more than 25,000 people, clothed 4,000, and gave medical supplies to some 3,000 more.

Salvatore's Italian Garden Restaurant in Lancaster replaced its expensive steaks with free sandwiches for all who jammed its doors. Owner Russ Salvatore "worked unselfishly all night," said one thankful patron. He fed more than 400 people, "and wouldn't accept any payment whatsoever."

The Greater Buffalo Regional Red Cross Office stayed

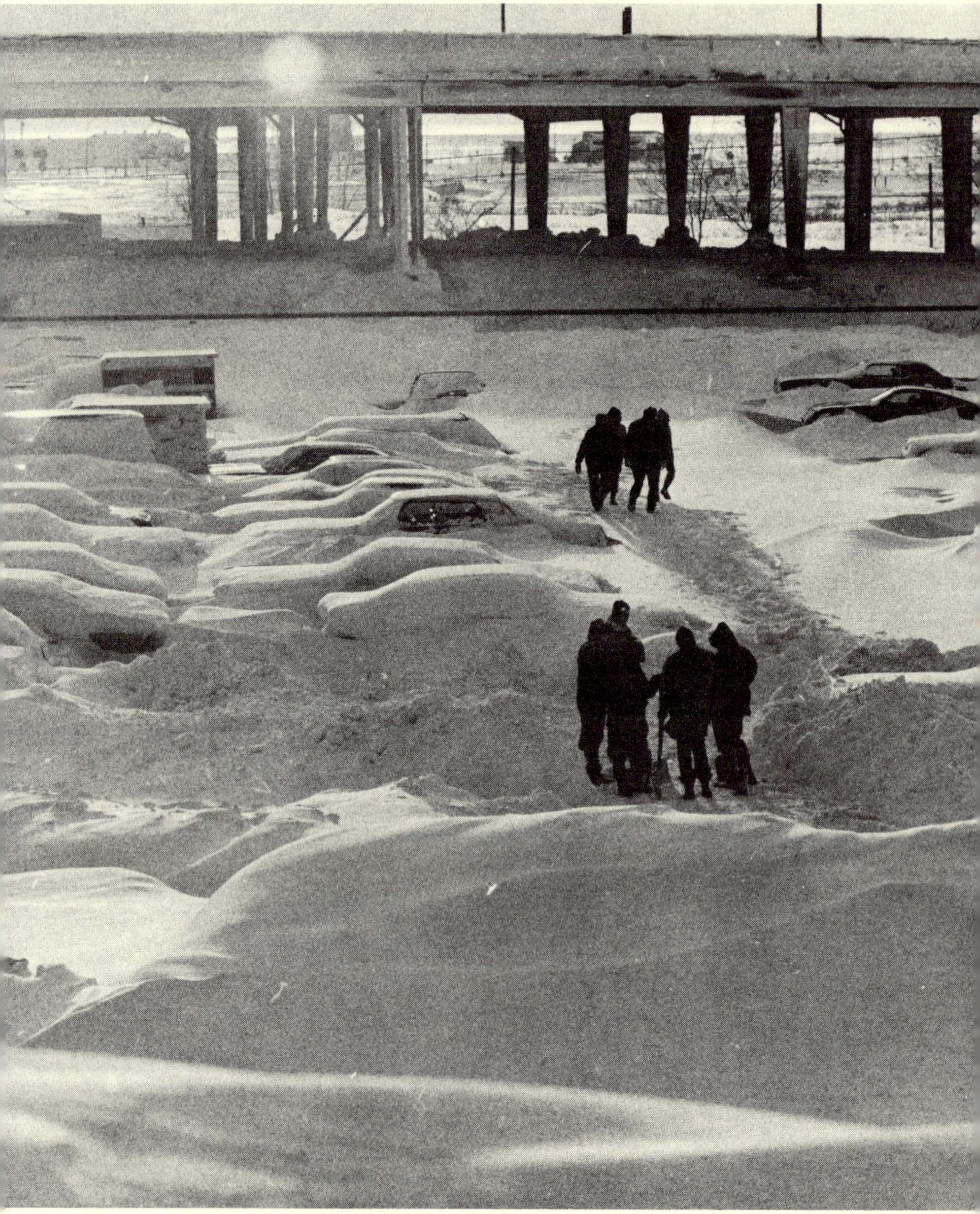

open all hours, making sure stranded victims could get the food and shelter they needed. Within the first few days after the storm struck, they had served more than 2,500 sandwiches and hundreds of gallons of coffee. They also managed to buy 250 loaves of bread from a nearby bakery to give to those in need.

The Buffalo News Building housed many people, supplying food and shelter. "For two days we were looked after, fed, and helped through an ordeal we never anticipated," said Lucy Morano, a grateful survivor.

The *Courier-Express* newspaper boys and girls made their deliveries, where possible, to give their subscribers some information and entertainment during the long, unpleasant days indoors. They also brought food, medicine, and other supplies to those in need, especially the elderly.

Other good neighbors plowed streets, driveways, and sidewalks and tried to get the automobiles running again. One truck driver drove at a snail's pace for two days to cover 2 miles (3.2 kilometers), bringing fuel to the elderly people at the Erie County Home and Infirmary.

Even though help and friendship were all around, some tragedies were bound to occur. A few were unavoidable. Five people were found frozen to death in their stalled cars, one within a five-minute walk of many warm houses.

For thirty-two hours, ambulances could go nowhere. "We couldn't get out to people," recalled Dr. Joseph Ziggi, "and they couldn't get in to us. I've never seen anything like it."

Stranded motorists camped out in office buildings when the January 1977 blizzards dumped snow on the Buffalo area.

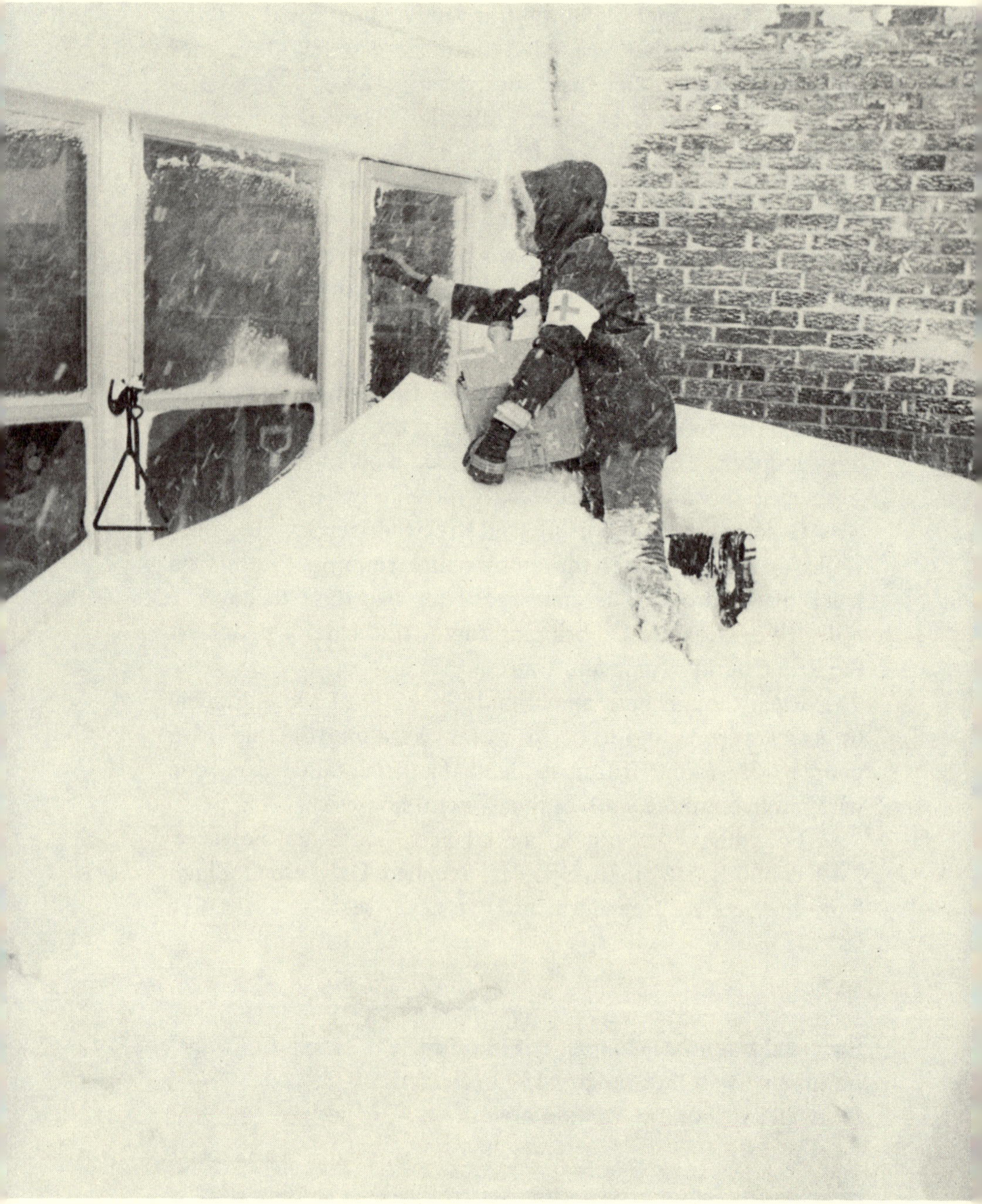

A fire in one house spread to eight others before heroic firemen could drag their hoses through four blocks of drifted roads.

While most of Buffalo's residents continued to be "good neighbors," there were some who used the blizzard as an opportunity to vandalize stores and homes. Some looting took place. And some abandoned automobiles were stolen. Vacant drugstores were robbed. Jewelry shops were burglarized. In one night, police arrested sixty thieves.

In many instances, good humor helped people get through situations they couldn't control. Employees who were unable to go home from work gathered in office buildings and the town hall, where they watched "Roots" and "Mary Hartman, Mary Hartman" on television.

Two young people stranded in one building played tic-tac-toe on a frosted window. And students didn't complain when the blizzard delivered an unexpected vacation from classes! Schools in most areas were closed for one to two weeks following the start of the storm.

But after several days at home, many families experienced "cabin fever." When parents and children were crowded together indoors for so many days, tempers grew short and everyone began getting on one another's nerves.

"These kids are driving me up the wall," said one mother of three.

Red Cross volunteers delivered emergency medical supplies and food to Buffalo residents who couldn't leave their homes because of high snowdrifts after the 1977 blizzards.

"I'm going stir-crazy," said a man who hadn't been able to get to work in a week.

"I'll be glad to get back to school," admitted one student.

By the end of the blizzard, most school districts were considering canceling or cutting short the planned Easter vacation and eliminating other holidays in order to make up the loss of schooldays. Bored pupils and anxious parents didn't object.

Even some animals experienced a few hours of freedom. Because of the large snowdrifts on the fences at the Buffalo Zoo, a number of deer escaped easily. But they were soon recaptured.

Help came quickly. "This city is fighting for its life," Buffalo's Mayor Makowski told President Carter. At the request of New York's governor Hugh Carey, on January 29 President Carter declared a regional state of emergency so that federal money could be used to save lives, remove the snow, and restore health and safety services.

The Federal Disaster Assistance Administration swung into action with orders from President Carter. At the FDAA's direction, the Army airlifted 300 men from an engineer task force at Fort Bragg, North Carolina, with snowblowers and trucks. And 500 National Guardsmen worked on the snowbanks.

The Air Force supplied giant C-130 cargo planes to airlift personnel, snow-removal equipment, spare parts, and cots and blankets from New York City, Washington, D.C., Colorado, and Michigan. The big planes landed every thirty minutes in Buffalo. After the life-saving tasks were underway, on February 5, President Carter declared nine counties a major disaster area. It was the first time in history that a disaster caused by a blizzard received this designation. This allowed local government, individuals, businesses, and farmers to get federal funds to help them recover. Some 300,000 people had been forced out of work.

The cost of the blizzard was staggering. The federal "price tag" was $93.2 million, including $18 million in city property damage and snow removal expenses.

But the "City of Good Neighbors" was not easily discouraged. Help and support turned good neighbors into fast friends, as everyone began stripping Buffalo of its winter blankets.

One new resident, Marcia Kelly, expressed the feelings of many old-time citizens when she commented on the "good neighbors" she had met during the storm.

Writing in the *Buffalo Evening News'* letters section, she thanked everyone for the help and friendship she had received. "Thank you, Buffalo. This is my first winter here, and in spite of all of the obvious drawbacks to this snowy season of 1977, I'm glad I decided to make this my home. . . ."

CHAPTER EIGHT

PREDICTING NATURAL DISASTERS AND HOW TO SURVIVE

Snow, wind, rain, water, and fire are among nature's wonders. But they can also result in disaster if they strike when people are unprepared. Each year, thousands of men, women, and children lose their lives in avalanches, volcanic eruptions, storms, and floods. No spot on earth is safe from their awesome power.

At the present time there is little we can do to prevent natural disasters. However, scientists are studying ways to predict them. And there are already many useful warning systems in effect that give citizens a chance to protect themselves from approaching danger.

One branch of the U.S. Department of Commerce specializes in studying the earth and sea and its many forces. It is the National Oceanic and Atmospheric Administration (NOAA), created in 1970. This organization combines experts from the National Ocean Survey, the National Environmental Satellite Service, and other groups. NOAA also communicates with and shares information with the U.S. Coast Guard. Together, these branches work to improve the safety and quality of life.

One important element of NOAA is the National Weather Service. Meteorologists in stations across the United States provide weather forecasts to the general public, as well as to groups involved in activities on water, on land, and in the air.

One of its most valuable services is the network of disaster warnings. The National Weather Service has outlined specific methods for dealing with tornadoes, hurricanes, floods, winter storms, tsunami, and other natural hazards of the earth and sea.

At NOAA's National Severe Storms Forecast Center in Kansas City, Missouri, Commerce Department weather personnel work seven days a week, twenty-four hours a day, studying and researching the conditions of the atmosphere that might lead to disasters.

The National Weather Service is alert to all kinds of destructive events and their possible harm to communities across the country. For this reason, they have developed the following warning systems for tornadoes, hurricanes, floods and winter storms.

SKYWARN

So far, there is no way to stop tornadoes. But they can be seen. And more lives can be saved. Tornadoes are best sighted by the human eye. Most tornadoes that are seen before they strike have been picked up by volunteer spotters.

This network of volunteers is a part of a project called SKYWARN, sponsored by the U.S. Commerce Department's Nationwide Natural Disaster Warning system. And it is a new element of the community tornado preparedness program of the National Weather Service.

The purpose of SKYWARN is to alert Americans to approaching hazards from the earth, sea, and sky, and to save lives during tornado emergencies. SKYWARN is a good example of what the individual, the family, the community, and government can do together to reduce the threat of tornadoes.

Even though this project is providing a much-needed service, it cannot be completely accurate all the time. There is always a chance that a tornado will not be spotted or that a report on one will not reach the National Weather Service in time to alert residents. However, both meteorologists and individual communities work together to improve this system.

Tornado watches are messages sent by the National Severe Storms Forecast Center to areas that may be in the path of a tornado. These *watches* tell people where and when the possible tornadoes are expected. Messages are teletyped directly to the local offices of the National Weather Service and sent to the public as quickly as possible over radio and television. Police, emergency groups, and volunteers also help get the information to residents promptly.

Tornado watches are not tornado warnings. Their purpose is to alert persons to the *possibility* of a tornado. Until a warning is issued, residents can continue their routines, but keep a watch for threatening weather.

Tornado warnings are sent out when a tornado has actually been sighted in the area or tracked by radar. Warnings give the location of the tornado, when it has been sighted, the areas where it is expected to move, and the time period it will take to strike. When a tornado warning is issued, residents must act quickly and take immediate safety precautions.

TORNADO SAFETY RULES

NOAA recommends that the following rules be observed when a tornado approaches:

1. In office buildings, go to an inside hallway on the lowest floor, or to the marked shelter area.
2. In homes, the basement offers the best safety. Curl up under sturdy furniture, if possible. If there is no basement, take cover in the center of the house, on the lowest floor, in a small room, closet, or bathroom, and keep some windows open but stay away from them.
3. In shopping centers, go to a marked shelter area (*not* to a parked car).
4. In schools, follow advance plans to an inside hallway on the lowest floor. If the building is not of reinforced construction, go to a nearby one that is, or take cover outside on low, protected ground. Stay out of auditoriums, gymnasiums, or other buildings with wide, free-span roofs.

5. In open country, move away from the tornado's path at right angles. If there is not time to escape, lie flat in the nearest ditch or ravine.
6. In mobile homes, move to the community shelter if one is available. If you are not in a mobile home park, leave your trailer or mobile home and take cover on low, protected ground.

HURRICANE HUNTERS

All year long, satellites alert meteorologists to changing weather systems. During summer and autumn, the Atlantic Hurricane Warning Service at the National Hurricane Center in Miami, Florida, and the Weather Service Hurricane Warning offices in New Orleans, San Juan, Washington, D.C., and Boston keep a special watch for tropical disturbances that might lead to hurricanes. Similar stations are located in San Francisco and Honolulu to watch for Pacific hurricanes.

When a storm begins to develop, an Air Force or Navy reconnaissance plane or one of NOAA's Research Flight Facility aircraft flies to the site of the storm and makes a full investigation. The flight crew records temperature pressure, takes wind readings, observes cloud formations, and notes the position and movement of the storm. These aircraft are referred to as "hurricane hunters" when they fly through the eye of the hurricane and deal with the storm's mighty force.

When a hurricane approaches the mainland, the Weather Service's radar fence picks it up and tracks its path. There are many overlapping radars installations from Texas to New England. Each station covers about 200 miles. A careful watch is also made at sea to forecast the arrival of destructive hurricane waves.

Hurricane watches mean that a hurricane is a real possibility. Residents are advised to go on as before but to be aware of further instructions and be prepared to move quickly if a warning is issued.

Hurricane warnings are sent if hurricane conditions are expected within twenty-four hours. These messages tell when and where winds of at least 74 mph (119 kph) are likely to occur. They also forecast unusually high waves or dangerously high water even if winds are less than hurricane force. These warnings are seldom issued more than twenty-four hours in advance. As soon as a warning is sent, residents are urged to take safety precautions quickly.

When a Hurricane Preparedness Committee suggests evacuation, people are asked to follow these procedures as soon as possible:

1. Shut off main gas valve and turn off main power switch before leaving home.
2. Head for the marked shelters or evacuation points in your area. Police and other officials will direct foot or auto traffic. Other instructions are available over the radio.
3. Take only what is absolutely necessary. Do not try to bring household equipment.
4. Follow Red Cross instructions at shelters and offer assistance.
5. Remain at the shelter until told that you may leave. Public Health officials and building inspectors will complete their inspection of affected areas before residents are released.

FLOODS, FLASH FLOODS, AND WARNINGS

NOAA keeps a round-the-clock, round-the-year check on our country's rivers. Through its National Weather Service, NOAA maintains a special river and rainfall reporting network. The flood warning service is an important part of the program, which deals with predicting other natural hazards as well. The warnings give people what they most need when disaster is about to strike—time, time to take action against loss of life and property.

The Weather Service's River Forecast Centers watch conditions and water levels at more than 2,500 points on rivers across the country. They measure stream flow, melting snow, soil conditions, and so on, in an effort to keep people informed of approaching danger.

River Forecast Centers issue flood forecasts and warnings when the rain that has fallen is enough to cause rivers to overflow their banks. Sometimes melting snow combines with rainfall to produce the same effect.

Flood watches are issued if conditions are expected to reach flood level. Residents are urged to listen for further information but to continue in their routine.

Early flood warnings allow residents to leave low-lying areas and move their personal belongings, livestock, and other possessions to high ground. Sometimes crops can be harvested ahead of time. And emergency organizations can also prepare to handle refugees and health hazards that usually come with floods.

Flood warnings are issued hours to days in advance. Messages and instructions are sent over radio and television and through local emergency agencies. The warning tells the expected degree of flooding (minor, moderate, or severe), the affected river, and when and where flooding will begin.

When heavy rains occur on watersheds of small streams, water levels may rise and produce *flash floods*. There is almost no time between detection and actual flooding in the case of flash floods. Prompt action is necessary to avoid death and destruction of property.

Flash floods can occur anywhere. Mountainous areas,

where torrential thunderstorm rains can change trickling brooks into raging rivers, are especially vulnerable. Buildings, cars, and parking lots are often deluged within seconds.

The National Weather Service has helped set up flash flood warning systems in about one hundred communities. But more are needed. Volunteers observe conditions and collect reports from the network. To be successful, a flash flood warning system requires the planning and cooperation of citizens in the communities affected.

Radar information from the National Weather Service and an alarm system tied in to the Weather Service facility are other methods that can help communities get the necessary information to their residents in time for them to seek shelter and safety.

Flash flood watches are issued when meteorologists receive word from the River Forecast Centers about the amounts of rainfall in their area that might cause flash flooding. The public is asked to be prepared and ready for immediate action if a flash flood warning is released.

Flash flood warnings are the most urgent kinds of weather warnings because residents must act *immediately*. When a flash flood warning is issued, it means the flooding is taking place at that moment.

People in the area of a flash flood are urged to leave as quickly as possible and to follow the Flood Safety Rules as recommended by NOAA:

Before the flood:
1. Keep on hand materials like sandbags, plywood, plastic sheets, and lumber.
2. Install check valves in building sewer traps to prevent floodwater from backing up.
3. Keep first-aid supplies handy.

4. Keep your automobiles fueled.
5. Keep a stock of food that does not require refrigeration.
6. Keep a portable radio, emergency cooking equipment, lights, and flashlights in working order.

When you receive a flood warning: *
7. Store drinking water in clean bathtubs and in other containers.
8. If time permits, move essential items to safe ground before leaving home; fill tanks so they will not float away and grease immovable machinery to lessen water damage.
9. Move to a safe area before floodwater cuts off the route.

During the flood
(for flash flood and seasonal flood areas):
10. Avoid areas subject to sudden flooding.
11. Do not try to cross a flowing stream where water is above your knees.
12. Do not try to drive over a flooded area—you can get trapped. If your car stalls, try to reach a safe place on foot. It is *not* safe to be inside a car when a flash flood strikes.

After the flood:
13. Do not use fresh food that has been touched by floodwaters.
14. Boil drinking water as a precaution.

---

* This applies to seasonal floods only. In the case of *flash flood warnings*, residents are urged to get to safety as swiftly as possible. There is not enough time to save belongings. Seconds can mean the difference between life and death.

15. Seek medical care at the nearest hospital. Food, shelter, clothing, and first aid are available at Red Cross centers.
16. Do not visit a disaster area; you could be in the way of emergency groups.
17. Do not handle live electrical equipment in wet areas; it should be checked and dried before returning to service.
18. Use flashlights, not lanterns or torches, to examine buildings. Highly flammable items such as leaking gas lines might be inside.
19. Report broken utility lines to the proper authorities. Do not go near them.

WINTER STORMS

Heavy snow warnings are issued when a fall of 4 inches (10 centimeters) or more is expected in a twelve-hour period, or a fall of 6 inches (15 centimeters) or more is expected in a twenty-four-hour period.

Blizzards are the most dramatic and dangerous of all winter storms. Low temperatures and strong winds carrying large amounts of blinding snow make up this most terrifying of all winter weather.

Blizzard warnings are issued when winds with speeds of at least 35 mph (56 kph) are accompanied by heavy falling or blowing snow that is expected to continue for a period of three hours or longer.

Severe blizzard warnings are issued when blizzards of extreme degrees are expected and bring winds of at least 45 mph (72 kph) plus heavy falling or blowing snow and a temperature of 10° F (−12° C) or lower.

NOAA's meteorologists work throughout the winter months at detecting the disturbances that may turn into severe winter storms. They also develop warnings against the approach of the storms.

NOAA suggests the following Winter Storm Safety Rules:

1. Check battery-powered equipment before the storm arrives. A portable radio or television may be the only contact you'll have with the outside world. Also check emergency cooking facilities and flashlights.
2. Check supply of heating fuel.
3. Check your food and stock an extra supply. Include foods that require no cooking or refrigeration, in case of power failure.
4. Prevent fire hazards due to overheated coal- or oil-burning stoves, fireplaces, heaters, or furnaces.
5. Stay indoors during storms.
6. Avoid prolonged snow shoveling. It can bring on a heart attack, one of the major causes of death during a blizzard.
7. Rural residents: Make necessary trips for supplies before the storm develops or not at all. Arrange for emergency heat supply in case of power failure. Be sure camp stoves and lanterns are filled.
8. Avoid using heating sources such as charcoal that deplete oxygen in the house.

Suggested winter storm car kit: Blankets or sleeping bags, matches and candles, empty 3-pound (1.35-kilogram) coffee can with plastic lid, facial tissue, paper towels, extra clothing, high-caloric nonperishable food, compass and road maps, knife, first-aid kit, shovel, sack of sand, flashlight or signal light, windshield scraper, booster cables, two tow chains, fire extinguisher, catalytic heater, and ax.

CHAPTER NINE

A LOOK AT THE FUTURE

At the present time, researchers are trying to improve the quality and safety of life by studying the nature of the earth and its elements. Scientists work every day at developing new methods and techniques that will lessen the loss of life and property that result from natural disasters. But there is still a great deal to learn. And there are many theories that have not been proven.

However, scientists continue their work in geological and seismological laboratories and in weather stations throughout the world. Here is a look at what they do.

TORNADO TRACKERS

Meteorologists have known for a long time that intense electrical activity accompanies most tornadoes. But it was not until 1973 that researchers at the federal government's Wave Propagation Laboratory in Boulder, Colorado, learned how this electrical activity works.

They found that a tornado fires off more "bursts" or clusters of electromagnetic impulses than any other type of storm. Sometimes there are as many as twenty a minute.

With this information, researchers developed a "tornado detector." This device lights up dramatically whenever a storm's electric activity reaches a tornado level at any distance within 50 miles (80 kilometers) of its antenna.

For several years, scientists have been testing these detectors in weather stations around the high-risk tornado areas. If they prove successful, they could give residents in threatened areas time to find shelter. This would save hundreds of lives each year.

HURRICANE HUNTERS

There is no proven method for preventing hurricanes. But research is being done to try and tame the violent storms. Hurricane hunter planes fly through trouble spots and "seed" the storm clouds with particles of silver iodide. This chemical is used to weaken their force.

Federal researchers have seeded several hurricanes and seemed to dampen some of the awesome energies of these giant storms. But at the present time, scientists agree that these seedings should be kept as experiments only. And they are careful to seed only those hurricanes that are far enough out at sea not to be a threat to areas where people live.

VOLCANO RESEARCH AND PREDICTION

There are volcano observatories throughout the world. In the United States, for example, the U.S. Geological Survey maintains a volcano observatory in Kilauea, Hawaii. For more than fifty years, volcanologists have studied the Kilauea volcano. They have measured the temperature and pressure of the gas, and they have studied the magnetic field of the volcano. They have also analyzed samples of lava by bringing it up through drill holes in special tubes. Lava is then run through a battery of tests and measurements in the observatory's geochemical laboratory.

The advance of volcanology is responsible for some ideas about how to predict an eruption. Scientists found that small earth tremors occur just before a volcano erupts. These tremors can be recorded on a seismograph. People can then be warned of the possibility of an eruption. At this time the method is not completely accurate, but more studies are being conducted.

Although we may never be able to change the forces of the earth, researchers hope that in the near future they will be able to predict volcanic eruptions with greater certainty. Meanwhile, they are also working to find ways to curb the flow of mud and lava once a volcano has erupted. This alone would save thousands of lives.

EARTHQUAKE RESEARCH AND PREDICTION

Peter Ward, chief of the prediction branch of the U.S. Geological Survey's earthquake research center at Menlo Park, California, said recently that at the present time it may be several decades before there's a proven system for predicting earthquakes. Some 200 to 250 people in our country are working on this project.

Scientists do feel, however, that we can cut down the loss of lives and the high damage to property by improving our construction standards. Most earthquake destruction is due to the collapse of unsound buildings.

Many structures in earthquake-prone areas are not built to withstand even a moderate quake. Structural engineers are now trying to deal with this problem.

Scientists in all parts of the world are working together on methods of prediction. To help them in their research, they collect and study information about earthquakes as they occur throughout the world.

Some researchers believe we can ease the destruction of large quakes by starting smaller ones. And some experiments have been done in this area. Holes are drilled into the face of a *fault*. Measured amounts of water are then pumped into the cracks between the rocks. The water makes the fault face slippery and adds weight to the rocks on one side of the fault. Rocks are then caused to slide a little way and to release some of the pressure that is building up. However, the results of these experiments are not definitive.

To help researchers in their work, the U.S. Geological Survey has a simple two-page questionnaire that they will mail to all zip codes surrounding epicenters of important earthquakes. Citizens can fill in the information about the time they felt the shock, where they were and what they were doing, and what effects they noticed, such as swaying fixtures, broken glass, or crumbled bricks.

Although a lot of work is being done to bring about predictions, some scientists wonder if they would even be that useful. Panic following an earthquake prediction might be worse than the quake itself. No one can be sure.

In the meantime, researchers struggle to come up with a method that will answer the three most important questions concerning an earthquake:

- When will it hit?
- Where will it happen?
- How powerful will it be?

Since there is no warning system in effect for earthquakes at this time, NOAA's safety rules offer guidelines for behavior during the shaking and afterwards:

During the shaking:
1. Don't panic. Keep calm and ride out the shaking.
2. If it catches you indoors, stay there. Take cover under a piece of sturdy furniture or in doorways, in halls, or against a side wall. Stay away from glass.
3. Don't use candles, matches, or other open flames either during or after the tremor. Douse all fires.
4. If you are outside during the quake, move away from buildings and utility wires. Stay in the open until the quaking stops.
5. Don't run through or near buildings. Falling debris is most dangerous near outer walls and just outside doorways.

6. If you are in a moving car, stop as quickly as safety permits, but stay in the car.

After the shaking:
1. Check your utilities, but do not turn them on. Earth movement may have cracked water, gas, and electrical conduits.
2. If you smell gas, open windows and shut off the main valve. Leave the building and report the gas leakage to authorities. Don't reenter until it is safe.
3. If water mains are damaged, shut off the supply at the main valve.
4. If electrical wiring is shorting out, close the switch at the main meter box.
5. Turn on radio or television (if conditions permit) to get the latest emergency bulletins.
6. Stay off the telephone except to report an emergency.
7. Don't go sight-seeing.
8. Stay out of severely damaged buildings; aftershocks can shake them down.

TSUNAMI PREDICTION

One dangerous aftermath of an earthquake is a tsunami (or harbor wave). This is one area of earthquake research, however, that has a reliable warning system. The Seismic Sea Wave Warning System is a network of warnings that can be sent out to people living far from the site of an earthquake. There are ten earthquake-recording stations and twenty wave-measuring stations in various parts of the Pacific Ocean. When these instruments record a quake on the ocean floor, a warning is sent to the governments of those countries likely to be hit. With several hours' notice, it is possible to move people away from the beaches. And many lives have been saved as a result.

AVALANCHE PREDICTION AND PREVENTION

In general, it is possible for experts to know when and where avalanches are likely to occur. Forecasting is also made easier because many avalanches descend on the same course year after year. Reports are then sent to threatened areas. In Switzerland, for example, bulletins are sent to the news media every Friday.

Sometimes snow avalanches are started *before* they reach dangerous levels. They can be triggered by artillery or mortar fire, rockets, or mines. Officials on some of the Swiss railways go out every morning before the traffic starts and direct fire at dangerous places on the higher snow slopes. Land mines are placed in position, and when the forecasting experts name the right time, they explode them electrically from a distance.

Part of avalanche prevention includes keeping dangerous snow masses from forming. Trees, growing close together as in a forest, provide the best defense. They help keep all but the worst avalanches from starting.

Artificial barriers are also built on some slopes. Rows of heavy walls are erected to break up the snow masses into small harmless sections. Houses are also constructed to withstand avalanches. Their sides face uphill like a wedge. A striking avalanche then splits—the two halves passing by the house without damage.

Railways and highways are protected by tunnels of built-up walls so that an avalanche will just slide over the structure.

Advances have been made in understanding and preventing much of the destruction and death brought about by these snow slides. But researchers agree there is still much to study and learn.

THE FUTURE OF FLOOD CONTROL

Scientists, engineers, government officials, and many other people spend their lives trying to protect citizens from the danger of floods. They attack the problem from many directions: control, prediction and warning, and relief to victims.

There are also programs established to improve standards for constructing buildings in areas that might flood. And new ways are being found to build houses and large buildings so they will not float off their foundations.

Waterproof coverings and windows and doors, electrical wires and appliances are all being improved so they can withstand the damage of water coverage.

In some areas where flooding is a routine occurrence, buildings on huge cement pillars are seen with their offices high above flood levels.

Another way to control flooding is to construct levees, dikes, and floodwalls to keep rivers from leaving their channels. Large rivers are also sometimes lined with high, manmade walls of dirt, sandbags, and cement.

Huge dams are also helpful because they block the natural flow of the rivers and hold their water in huge lakes. When the heavy water flow comes down the river, it can be held and then released at a later time. And the lakes behind these dams can also be used for recreational purposes, to supply water to towns and industries, and to irrigate farmland.

Scientists have also worked at finding ways to lower the amount of runoff. One way is to keep the soil carefully planted with a cover of plants and shrubs. And another way is to build small ponds to catch and hold the heavy runoff of water in reserve until it can soak into the soil instead of running off into the streams. But in spite of all the preventive measures, rivers continue to flood and many people suffer each year. That is why the best protection is good prediction and warning.

SUGGESTIONS FOR FURTHER READING

Bova, Ben. *Man Changes the Weather*. Reading, Mass.: Addison-Wesley, 1973.

Brindze, Ruth. *Hurricanes: Monster Storms from the Sea*. New York: Atheneum, 1973.

Brown, Billye, and Walter R. *Historical Catastrophes: Volcanoes*. Reading, Mass.: Addison-Wesley, 1970.

―――. *Historical Catastrophes: Hurricanes and Tornadoes*. Reading, Mass.: Addison-Wesley, 1972.

―――. *Historical Catastrophes: Earthquakes*. Reading, Mass.: Addison-Wesley, 1974.

―――. *Historical Catastrophes: Floods*. Reading, Mass.: Addison-Wesley, 1975.

Herbert, Don, and Fulvio Bardossi. *Kilauea: Case History of a Volcano*. New York: Harper & Row, 1968.

Lauber, Patricia. *Earthquakes*. New York: Random House, 1972.

Navarra, John Gabriel. *Nature Strikes Back*. Garden City, N.Y.: Natural History Press, 1971.

INDEX

Agung, Mount (Bali), 16, 17, 20, 23, 24, 25
Alaska, 28, 31, 35, 38
Ash volcanic, 17, 19, 20, 21, 24
Atlantic Ocean, 23, 37, 59, 63
Avalanche, 2, 6–13, 24, 46–47, 94, 111–112

Bali, island of, 16, 21, 23, 24, 25
Besakih, temple of, 16, 20, 24, 25
Blizzard 2, 82–91
    warning, 84, 102
Boulders, giant, 23–24, 49
Buffalo, New York, 82–83, 84, 85, 90, 91

Casualties, 2, 12–13, 16–17, 21, 25, 35, 51, 55, 57, 64–65, 68–69, 71, 79, 83, 94
Clouds, 47, 63, 73, 83–84, 97
Conduit, volcanic, 17, 19
Crater, volcanic, 16, 17, 24
Crust, earth's, 17, 23, 28, 29, 46
Cyclone, 61, 63, 84

Dams, 2, 42, 43, 112
Destruction,
    avalanche, 6–7, 10–12, 112

Destruction *(continued)*
　earthquake, 2, 33, 35
　flood, 20, 42, 46–47, 49–50, 64
　hurricane, 55–57, 58–59, 64
　tornado, 68–73, 77–79
　tsunami, 38
　volcanic eruption, 17, 19–20, 21–25

Earthquake, 2, 28–39, 46, 108–09, 110
　causes, 28–29
　San Francisco (1906), 2
　undersea, 38, 43
Eka Dasa Rudra (festival), 16, 24–25
Emergency aid, 13, 21–23, 38, 65, 79, 90–91
Emergency relief organizations, 58, 65, 79, 85, 99, 102
Epicenter, earthquake, 29, 31, 109
Evacuation, 21, 24, 55, 98, 99, 100–101, 110–111

Federal Disaster Assistance Administration (FDAA), 79, 90
Flood, 2, 12, 20, 42–51, 58–59, 64, 65, 94, 95
　causes, 43, 45–46
　control, 112–13
　flash, 99–100
　warnings, 98–102, 112

Gases, volcanic, 19–20, 107
Geologists, 29, 45, 51, 106
Glaciers, 6, 7
Gulf of Mexico, 54, 55, 59
Gulfport, Mississippi, 54, 57–59

Hurricane, 2, 43, 61, 77, 94, 95
　Camille, 54–65
　causes, 61–63
　cloud seeding, 107
　eye, 61, 97
　hunters, 54, 97, 106–107
　path, 63, 97
　preparation for, 57–58
　season, 61, 97
　warnings, 54, 55, 65, 97–98

Landslide, 7, 10, 42, 45, 46–47, 64
Lava, 17, 19, 24, 107–108
Los Angeles, Basin, 43, 47

Magma, 16–17
Meteorologists, 46, 47, 63, 73, 85, 94, 95, 97, 100, 102, 106

Mud slides, 21–24, 46–47, 50–51, 108

National Oceanic and Atmospheric Administration (NOAA), 94, 96–98, 100, 102, 103, 109
National Severe Storms Forecast Center, 94, 95
National Weather Service, 46, 47, 54, 55, 73, 82–85, 94–95, 96–100

Pacific Ocean, 12, 23, 35, 38, 46, 61, 84, 97, 110
Pass Christian, Mississippi, 55, 58, 65
Peru, 6–13
Prediction, 2, 94–103
    avalanche, 7, 111
    earthquake, 108–09
    flood, 46–47, 50–51, 99–100, 112
    tornado, 71–73
    volcanic eruptions, 107–108

Radar, 54, 96, 97, 100
Rain, 2, 43, 45–47, 58, 61, 63–64, 94, 98–100
Ranrahirca (Peru), 6, 7, 11, 12, 13
Red Cross, 65, 85–87, 98, 102

Richter scale, 37–38
Ring of fire, 23, 35

Safety rules,
    earthquake, 109–110
    flood, 100–102
    hurricane, 98
    tornado, 96–97
    winter storm, 103
Salvation Army, 65, 85
Satellite photographs, 46, 54, 97
Seaquakes, 38, 43, 110. *See also* Tsunami
Seismic waves, 29, 31, 38
Seismograph, 31, 106–107
SKYWARN, 95–96
Snow, 43, 82–85, 90, 94, 99, 111
    types, 10–11
    warnings, 102
Southern California, 42, 43, 45, 49, 51
Storms, 2, 46, 47, 54, 57, 59–61, 63–64, 69, 73, 97, 106–107
    winter, 83–84, 94–95, 102–103
Survivors, 12–13, 20–21, 35, 38–39, 58–59, 71, 87

Thunderstorms, 47, 69, 100
Tides, high, 2, 55, 59, 61

Tornado, 2, 57, 68–79, 94, 97
   causes, 69, 106
   preparedness program, 95–96
   speed of, 68, 69, 73
   warnings, 71, 73, 95–96
"Tornado Alley," 69, 106
Trade winds, 63
Tsunami, 38, 43, 94, 110–111

Victims, 3, 6, 7, 10–13, 19–21, 33, 35, 46–47, 49–50, 55, 64–65, 68–69, 78, 83, 85–87

Volcano, 108
   eruptions, 2, 16–25, 94, 107
   types, 23

Warning systems, 47–49, 94–97, 100, 102, 109–110
Waves, high, 2, 43, 55, 61, 97, 98, 110
Winds, high, 2, 71, 94
   blizzard, 82–83, 84, 102
   hurricane, 54–59, 61, 63, 64, 97, 98
   tornado, 68–69, 71, 73, 77–78